A Quick Index to Twenty Essential Questions

10. Special equipment
What special equipment is required and what are its space requirements?
154, 214, 218, 221

11. Materials
What materials need to be uniquely considered or rejected?
93, 98, 124, 126, 129, 182, 204, 228, 241–42, 245

12. Acoustic control
What special acoustic and other sound control considerations affect the design?
154

13. Lighting design
What special lighting (day and artificial) considerations affect the design?
2, 8, 19, 27–30, 53–54, 60, 64–65, 67–68, 74, 78, 81, 86–87, 89, 93–96, 115, 127, 131, 138, 140, 149, 151, 154, 175, 177, 182, 192, 217, 233, 235, 237–41, 245–47, 250–51

14. Interiors issues
What special considerations determine the planning of interiors (scale, color, texture of finishes, furnishings, special features)? Fire and smoke protection.
2, 27, 29, 54, 60, 64–65, 93–94, 97, 101, 114–15, 131, 143, 147, 157, 162, 183, 192, 193, 211, 236, 242, 246–47

15. Wayfinding
What special factors determine graphics, signing, and wayfinding?
2, 14, 18, 60, 68, 74, 101, 143, 147, 157, 177, 182–83, 190, 192, 204, 235

16. Additions/renovation/restoration/adaptive reuse
What are the special concerns when renovating a facility? (Consider: restoration; functional/infrastructure retrofit; adaptive reuse)
39, 48, 78, 89, 95, 101, 187–88, 214, 228, 242, 244

17. International challenges
On international work in this building type, what anomalies arise to influence marketing, design, presentations, document production, correspondence, field presence, billing?
124, 162

18. Operation and maintenance
What are the special procedures for operating and maintaining the completed facility?
250–52

19. Key cost factors
What are the typical costs for construction, including furnishings, fixtures, and equipment? Because of variability in program, there are no reliable guidelines for the costs of museum construction. Many institutions include very expensive exhibit installation in the cost of construction, for example, to the point where the cost of the installation may exceed that of the building

20. Finances, fees, feasibility
What are the typical techniques for financing this facility?
40, 45, 68, 74, 101, 124, 162

BUILDING TYPE BASICS FOR

museums

Stephen A. Kliment, Series Founder and Editor

ARTHUR ROSENBLATT
RKK&G Museum and Cultural Facilities Consultants

JOHN WILEY & SONS, INC.

New York, Chichester, Weinheim, Brisbane, Singapore, Toronto

Other titles in the
BUILDING TYPE BASICS
series

HEALTHCARE FACILITIES
Michael Bobrow and Julia Thomas; Thomas Payette;
Ronald Skaggs; Richard Kobus

ELEMENTARY AND SECONDARY SCHOOLS
Bradford Perkins

This book is printed on acid-free paper. ☺

Copyright © 2001 by John Wiley & Sons, Inc. All rights reserved.

Published simultaneously in Canada.

Interior design and layout: Jay Anning, Thumb Print

Library of Congress Cataloging-in-Publication Data:
Rosenblatt, Arthur.
    Building type basics for museums/by Arthur Rosenblatt.
       p.   cm.
    Includes index.
    ISBN 0-471-34915-1 (cloth : alk paper)
    1. Museum buildings—Designs and plans. I. Title.
    NA6690 .R67 2000
    727.6—dc21

                      00—43328

Printed in the United States of America.

10 9 8 7 6 5 4

CONTENTS

FOREWORD

Arthur Rosenblatt is the only architect I've ever met who cares as deeply about the humanity of a job as he does about the common sense and quality of design and the sanctity of the budget.

His early park designs in the 1960s are virtual portraits of the complex community for which they were created. Because of them, when I was appointed Parks Commissioner of the City of New York, I made him chief architect of that massive system. Arthur became the indispensable man who lifted recreational design out of the old Bob Moses chain-link-fence-swing-and-to-hell-with-kids abyss. He worked tirelessly with a cadre of young adventure-playground architects and mothers to make sure that the designs not only won architectural awards but worked perfectly for the kids.

When I took off to become director of the Metropolitan Museum of Art, I enlisted Arthur to help carry out the architectural Master Plan that would transform that institution and begin to change the face of museums for all time. He personally chose for me as architects the firm of Kevin Roche, John Dinkeloo and Associates. I'd just seen their new museum complex in Oakland, California, which had had some birthing problems. His tart and typical answer to my moaning and groaning was: "Because they've done it once, they'll never do it again." And they didn't; the MMA's huge expansion was surprisingly and gratifyingly free of difficulties.

Arthur swore that Roche, Dinkeloo would definitely see to it that the doubling of the museum from seven to fourteen acres, the restoration of the 1,000-foot façade and Fifth Avenue plaza, the renovation of countless galleries, the building of five wings, plus the first underground visitors' parking garage smack in Central Park, would come in on (or under) budget. "Yeah, sure," I thought to myself. Yet his word, as usual, was good. Budget: $500 million. The work was completed on budget—and on time.

Among my favorite memories of those days are the many times Arthur would bustle into my office at the museum, drill his eyes into mine, and say, "Tommy, are you really going to do this stupid thing?"

Invariably, thank goodness, I didn't.

THOMAS HOVING
New York, January 2000

PREFACE

STEPHEN A. KLIMENT, *Series Founder and Editor*

This book on museum planning and design is one of the first in Wiley's "Building Type Basics" series on principal building types. It is not a coffee-table book lavish with color photography but meager in usable content. Rather, it contains the kind of instant information architects, and consultants, and their clients need in their various kinds of work, where, inevitably, time is scarce. As architectural practice becomes more generalized and firms pursue and accept design commissions for a widening range of building types, the books in this series will offer a convenient hands-on resource providing basic information on the initial design phases of a project, and answers to the questions design professionals routinely encounter in these crucial early stages. Members of museum boards, museum directors, registrars and curators, as well as architect selection committees, will also discover helpful information as they screen architects for museum commissions.

After a period of decline, reflecting stagnant public interest in viewing art and in expressing cultural heritage, museum construction took a sharp upturn in the 1980s as the public in the United States and overseas took a new interest in that heritage. The result was the building of a gargantuan volume of museums of every type, character, and size. And converting this consciousness into bricks and mortar became a lot easier as the economies in many nations, especially in the United States, flourished, making ample dollars available to sustain the trend. The funding came from private patrons, from scores of eleemosynary organizations and, often, from public moneys amassed from soaring tax revenues.

The cycle is unlikely to end any time soon. Even modest sized communities see it as a matter of pride to possess a museum of some sort, whether it is to display art or the sciences, express a strong local ethnic birthright, or to serve as a habitat for plants and animals.

Two vital components in this upsurge of interest in museums have been, and will continue to be, pressures to retrofit existing museums for climate, lighting and security, and to build additions to museums—some of them almost rivaling their original structure in size—to accommodate the vast upsurge in the size and range of collections.

Finally, every designer and museum board member recognizes that today's museum is no longer just a place for art cognoscenti to gather and admire art. On the contrary, the typical museum of the 20th century became a bustling combination of destination site and tourist attraction. Such a place, aside from showing original art, now provides places to eat, to buy souvenirs and reproductions, and to view virtual showings of real art in electronic formats. To meet these demands, and to survive the tough competition among museums for visitors, museums have taken to airing blockbuster shows, which alone have had a dramatic impact on planning and design.

To make it simpler for readers of this book to find what they want, author Arthur Rosenblatt, architect, eminent museum consultant and overseer of the huge expansion program of New York's Metropolitan Museum of Art, has broken up this building type into several categories. These are:

- Art museums

- History museums

- Children's museums

- Science and natural history museums

- Specialized museums and galleries

The book follows a format that has become the hallmark of the series. The subject matter is tightly organized for ease of use. The heart and soul of the volumes is a set of Twenty Questions most frequently asked about a building type, above all in the early phases of its design. The Twenty Questions cover such topics as predesign, circulation, unique design concerns, site planning, codes and access, energy and environmental challenges, structure, mechanical, and electrical systems, information technology, materials, acoustics and lighting issues, interiors, wayfinding, additions, renovation and retrofit issues, and matters of operation and maintenance, and financing. Cost issues are not covered due to the tremendous variations among big city, regional, and overseas museum venues.

Mr. Rosenblatt has explored and supplied solutions to the applicable Twenty Questions, using lean text plus tables, diagrams, drawings and photo illustrations. For the convenience of readers, an index tied to the Twenty Questions is printed on the end papers in front of the book and at the back.

This volume examines the issues and concerns raised by the Twenty Questions by presenting a group of twenty-five recently completed museums. Included are design lessons to be learned from such large well-known venues as the Rose Center for Earth and Space, New York, Getty Museum, Los Angeles, and the Guggenheim Museum, Bilbao, all the way to smaller or less well-known spots such as the Kiasma Museum, Helsinki and the Route 66 Museum, Clinton, Oklahoma. Each museum account begins with a brief listing of the design challenges encountered and met by that museum, followed by text and a generous array of drawings, charts, tables, sketches and photographs about each project.

To round out the volume, the author has written a series of "notes" that take up concerns unique to museums. They are: lighting, mechanical/electrical and environmental systems; security; and fire protection.

I hope, as you plunge into this book, that it will serve you as guide, reference, and inspiration.

ACKNOWLEDGMENTS

This book could not have been completed without the assistance of a good number of people.

First of all, I would like to thank my wife, Ruth Benjamin, for her constant encouragement and editorial guidance, despite a commitment to her own writing responsibilities.

I would also like to express appreciation to my partners at RKK&G, Nicholas Koutsomitis and Maria Cristina Gomez, for their understanding and support while maintaining a busy architectural practice.

Stephen Kliment, editor of the entire Building Type Basics series, provided the sense of purpose and pace necessary for keeping the project on track.

Amanda L. Miller, at John Wiley & Sons, gave me invaluable direction and support.

Thanks are also due members of my family, Judy Rosenblatt, Paul Rosenblatt, and Petra Fallaux, for their patience with me during the past year.

And, of course, boundless credit is due the architects, designers, and photographers of the projects that appear in this book.

ART
MUSEUMS

GRAND LOUVRE, *Paris, France*

I. M. PEI & PARTNERS, PEI COBB FREED & PARTNERS, ARCHITECTS (1989/1993)

Background and Purpose

Begun in 1202 as the fortified castle of Philippe Auguste and transformed into the palace of virtually every French king thereafter, the 800-year-old complex of the Louvre chronicles the history of France in stone. The buildings, a series of royal residences, were ill suited to serve as a museum, however. With only a fraction of the 40 percent support space now considered mandatory for museums, the Louvre was, as I. M. Pei says, "a theater with no backstage."

The challenge for President François Mitterand in 1981 was to renovate and significantly expand this national monument, enhance its links to the City of Paris, and vastly improve the museum for public use—all without destroying the landmark architecture of the palace or interrupting its daily operations.

Site Plan and Circulation

Phases I and II of the solution involved these key elements:

- Reorganization of the U-shaped museum around a focal courtyard. The striking Louvre Pyramid in the seven-acre Cour Napoléon becomes the new public entrance to the museum.

- Visitors entering through the Pyramid emerge onto the Belvedere, a projecting triangular balcony that looks down into the main lobby, or Halle Napoléon (Great Hall), and out through the Pyramid to an unobstructed view of the palace and the sky. The Belvedere disperses crowds by means of two escalators and a

helicoidal staircase that spirals down to the main lobby. In addition, an open cylindrical elevator rises and descends pistonlike without lateral support.

- The Halle Napoléon (lobby/Great Hall), the museum's reception area, is a skylit public square that can be enjoyed without admission to the exhibition galleries. Surrounded by information desks and automated ticket dispensers, its four sides lead to the following areas:

(*text continues on page 6*)

SIGNIFICANT ISSUES

Program
To restore and enlarge the museum, improving services and opening more of its collection to the public

Circulation
Bringing order to a historically inaccessible structure

Unique design concerns
How to modernize one of France's greatest landmarks

Site planning
Conveying pedestrians and vehicles to a difficult site

Lighting design
Introduction of controlled natural light

Interior issues
Protecting historic interior spaces

Wayfinding
Orienting the visitor within a complex plan

Grand Louvre

The Pyramid at night.
Photo: Deide Von Schawen

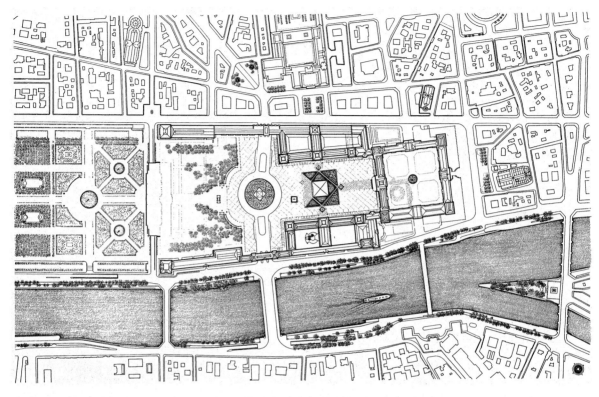

▲ Site plan of Grand Louvre, Paris.

◄ View of Pyramid at the main entrance.

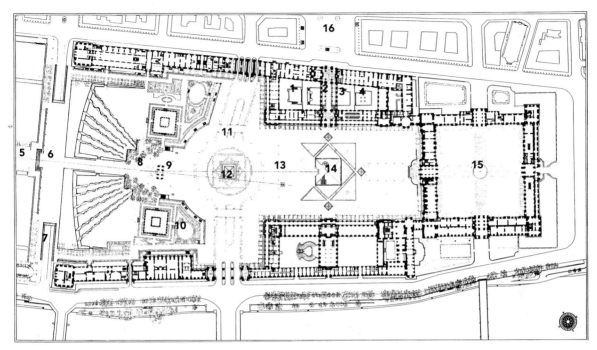

▲ Key to Grand Louvre
1 *Cour Marly*
2 *Passage Richelieu*
3 *Cour Puget*
4 *Cour Khorsabad*
5 *Jardin des Tuileries*
6 *Terrasse Tuileries*
7 *Général Lemonnier Underpass*
8 *Jardin du Carrousel*
9 *L'Arc du Carrousel*
10 *Abords du Palais*
11 *Rond Point Carrousel*
12 *Pyramide Inversée*
13 *Cour Napoléon*
14 *Pyramid/Main Entrance*
15 *Cour Carrée*
16 *Place du Palais Royale*

▶ View from Grand Louvre toward the Tuileries.

A 420-seat multiuse auditorium
An orientation center for children and
  group visits
Restaurants and cafés
A bookstore

- A half-mile-long expansion building, constructed under the courtyard, serves as a bridge for the Louvre's wings and provides greatly needed museum services and public amenities. Once a barrier to circulation, this building has become a vital connective tissue with pedestrian links to the surrounding city. A new underground vehicular network helps to relieve congestion around the museum.

- Conversion of the Richelieu Wing from the Ministry of Finance into exhibition space. Six floors of dingy government offices were demolished. Within the historic shell structure, and to coincide with the original façade, the interior has been rebuilt into three levels for:
Sculpture
Decorative arts
Painting galleries

- Spaces between public areas are devoted to:
Visitor services
Staff facilities
Museum storage

SUMMARY OF THE RESTORATION AND EXPANSION OF THE LOUVRE

	Area (sq ft)		Area (sq ft)
Phase I		Information areas	17,000
Entrance Pyramid (Cour Napoléon)		Reception, circulation, cafés	23,600
Plaza pyramids		Technical	116,800
Halle Napoléon		Islamic art	13,500
Belvedere (grade level)	3,130	French sculpture	108,600
Mezzanine	224,640	Eastern antiquities	30,300
Main recreation hall	268,920	Decorative arts	52,600
Technical level	172,800	Painting collections	
Total building area	669,490	French painting	10,500
		Northern European painting	37,600
Phase II		Salle Rubens	72,300
Richelieu Wing	348,400	Related spaces	
Public areas	235,500	Underground parking	80 spaces
Permanent exhibition	188,300	Staff parking	180 spaces
Temporary exhibition	2,600	Public parking	620 spaces

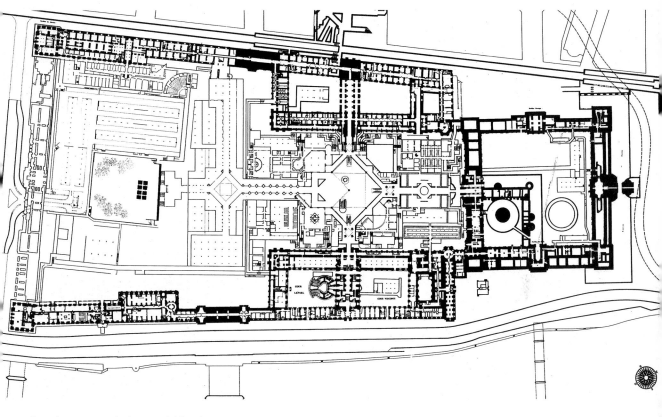

Plan of Concourse (below grade) level.

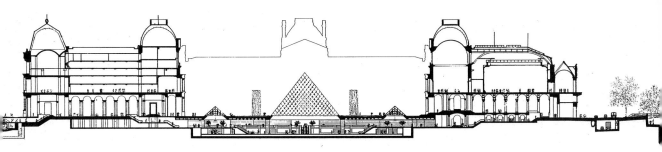

Section through Louvre.

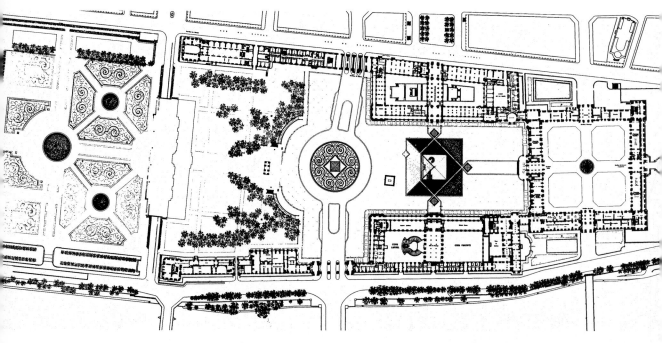

Plan of ground (entry) level.

Lighting

The restored Richelieu Wing is penetrated by three skylit sculpture courts. The skylights regulate the distribution and amount of light admitted into the galleries. They are composed of:

- A top layer of translucent glass with a polyvinyl filter to absorb destructive ultraviolet rays

- Egg-crate-like screens of inclined white aluminum blades to prevent the entry of direct sunlight

- A bottom layer of white plaster fins to reflect light and direct it onto the walls

Supplementary lighting is provided by artificial sources installed out of view, in reflective trays set into the upper surface of the white plaster fins.

Visitor Programs

In past years, the museum received some three million visitors annually. With completion of the modernization project, that number exceeded five million and was still growing. To accommodate this increase, the Louvre expanded its visitor services program. In the Richelieu Wing there are:

- Eight rest areas

- Information centers within exhibition spaces

- Two new restaurants

- Rest rooms on each floor

- Six escalators

- Handicapped lifts and elevators

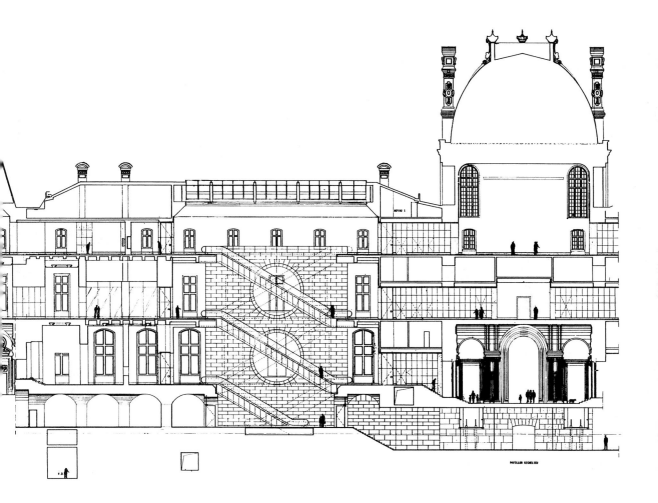

Section through new
enclosed courtyard. Note
glass (skylight) roof over
courtyard.

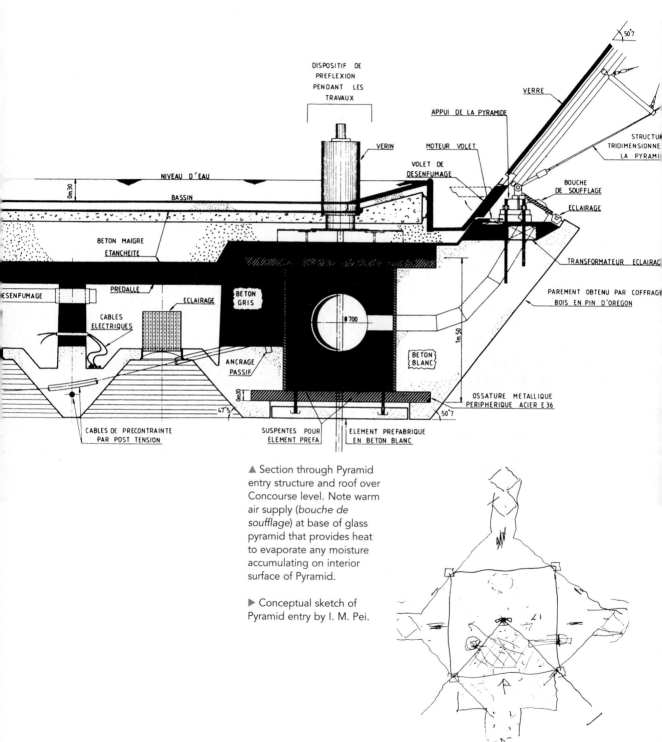

DISPOSITIF DE PREFLEXION PENDANT LES TRAVAUX

VERRE

APPUI DE LA PYRAMIDE

STRUCTUR TRIDIMENSIONNE LA PYRAMI

VERIN

MOTEUR VOLET

VOLET DE DESENFUMAGE

BOUCHE DE SOUFFLAGE

ECLAIRAGE

NIVEAU D´EAU

0m 30

BASSIN

BETON MAIGRE ETANCHEITE

TRANSFORMATEUR ECLAIRAC

DESENFUMAGE

PREDALLE

BETON GRIS

CABLES ELECTRIQUES

ECLAIRAGE

ANCRAGE PASSIF

Ø 700

1m 50

BETON BLANC

PAREMENT OBTENU PAR COFFRAGE BOIS EN PIN D´OREGON

0m 10

47°5

OSSATURE METALLIQUE PERIPHERIQUE ACIER E 36

50°7

CABLES DE PRECONTRAINTE PAR POST TENSION

SUSPENTES POUR ELEMENT PREFA

ELEMENT PREFABRIQUE EN BETON BLANC

▲ Section through Pyramid entry structure and roof over Concourse level. Note warm air supply (*bouche de soufflage*) at base of glass pyramid that provides heat to evaporate any moisture accumulating on interior surface of Pyramid.

▶ Conceptual sketch of Pyramid entry by I. M. Pei.

Entry to the Grand Louvre
on a typical day.
Photo: Leonard Jacobson

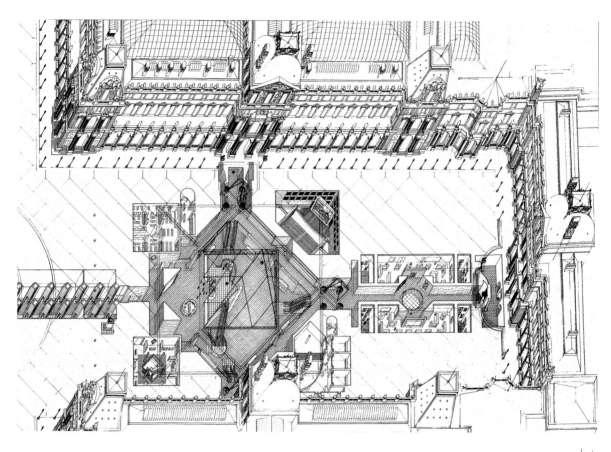

▲ Exploded view of
Concourse level below
Pyramid entrance.

▶ Section through
renovated gallery. Note new
skylight admitting controlled
natural light. Louvers and
new ceiling construction
provide distribution of light.

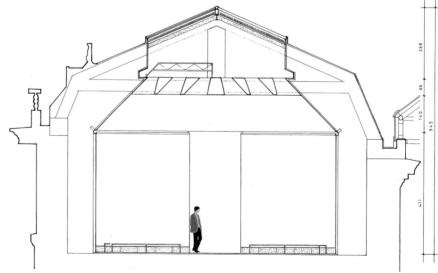

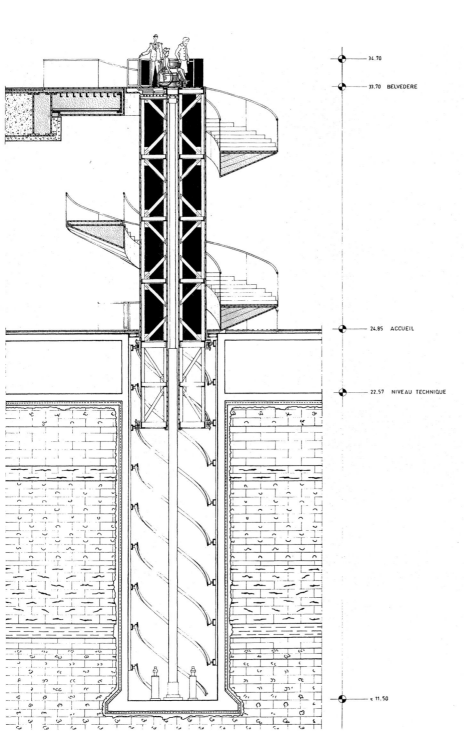

34.70

33.70 BELVEDERE

24.85 ACCUEIL

22.57 NIVEAU TECHNIQUE

≈ 11.50

Section through the helicoidal staircase within the Pyramid entrance. The stair spirals down to the main lobby (Concourse level) with no armature apparent. In the central void of the spiral, a cylindrical elevator rises and descends pistonlike without lateral support.

THE GETTY CENTER, *Brentwood, Los Angeles, California*
RICHARD MEIER AND PARTNERS, ARCHITECT (1997)

Site
The Getty Center unites the J. Paul Getty Museum and the Getty Trust's scholarly, conservation, administrative, and grant programs on one site. Located in the foothills of the Santa Monica Mountains, the 110-acre campus with its extensive gardens attracted more than 1.4 million visitors in its first year.

Severe zoning restrictions limited the possible size and height of the buildings. Most of them are arranged along two natural ridges that form the boundaries of the site.

Circulation
Visitors enter the Getty Center through the main gate at the north end of the campus. Those arriving by car park in a six-floor, 1,200-car underground garage or a second smaller facility. Then they are taken by tram to the large glass-walled entrance hall at the arrival plaza, where they may view a ten-minute orientation film in one of two small theaters and decide whether to enter the museum immediately or explore the site first.

Principal spaces
The entrance hall also contains:

- A 450-seat auditorium, equipped for lectures, films, symposia, and musical programs

- An information desk

- A book/gift shop

A cluster of five two-story pavilions, connected and bridged by walkways on both levels, houses:

- Four pavilions of permanent collections, presented chronologically

- Twenty-two skylit painting galleries on the upper level

- Gallery displays on the courtyard level including:
  Sculpture
  Illuminated manuscripts of the Middle Ages and Renaissance
  Drawings by major artists
  Glass
  Ceramics
  French and other European furniture
  Decorative arts (installed in 14 galleries designed by Thierry Despont to evoke the styles of Louis XIV and his successors)
  More than 65,000 photographs

SIGNIFICANT ISSUES

Program
Creation of a vast, encyclopedic museum

Unique design concerns
Finding a unified contemporary design for a group of museum and museum-related structures

Site planning/parking
A relatively remote and inaccessible site creating problems of access and parking

Wayfinding
The need to provide visual orientation for the visitor within a complex campus of buildings

---

Exterior view
Photo: Scott Frances/Esto

PRINCIPAL SPACES

	Area (sq ft)
The J. Paul Getty Museum	157,534
Offices	13,534
Exhibition space	80,000
Entry hall and associated spaces	4,300
Cafeteria	2,000
Bookshop	2,200
Library	2,000
Restoration workshop	1,200
Storerooms for	
Three-dimensional art	5,000
Two-dimensional art	3,000
Paper and flat art	1,000
General supplies and equipment	11,000
Maintenance and shops	11,000
Circulation and miscellaneous	21,300
The Getty Research Institute for the History of Art and the Humanities, with	
Work spaces for 150 staff and 200 scholars	
A library of more than 700,000 volumes	
Two million study photographs	
Rare books, monographs, and archival material	201,000
The Getty Conservation Institute	
The Getty Education Institute for the Arts	
The Getty Trust	80,000
The Getty Information Institute and Administrative Offices	64,000
A 450-seat Auditorium	31,000
Restaurant/café	29,000
Total	**720,068**

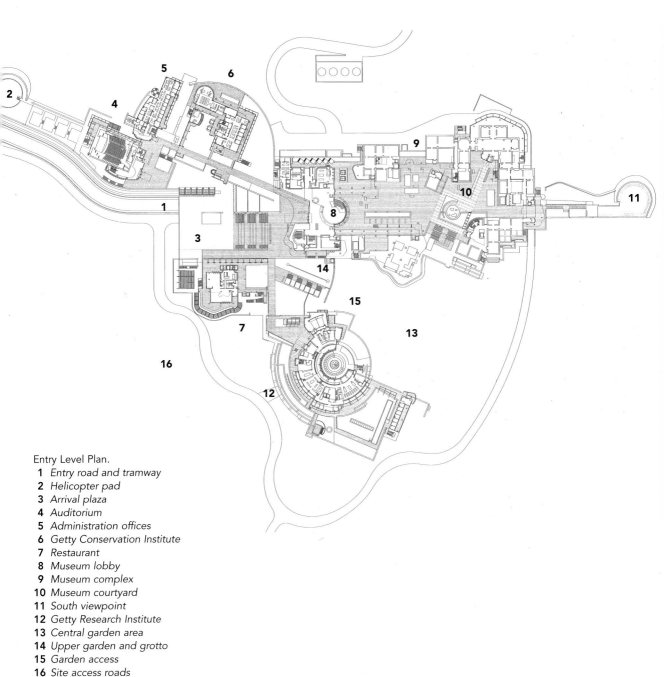

Entry Level Plan.
1 Entry road and tramway
2 Helicopter pad
3 Arrival plaza
4 Auditorium
5 Administration offices
6 Getty Conservation Institute
7 Restaurant
8 Museum lobby
9 Museum complex
10 Museum courtyard
11 South viewpoint
12 Getty Research Institute
13 Central garden area
14 Upper garden and grotto
15 Garden access
16 Site access roads

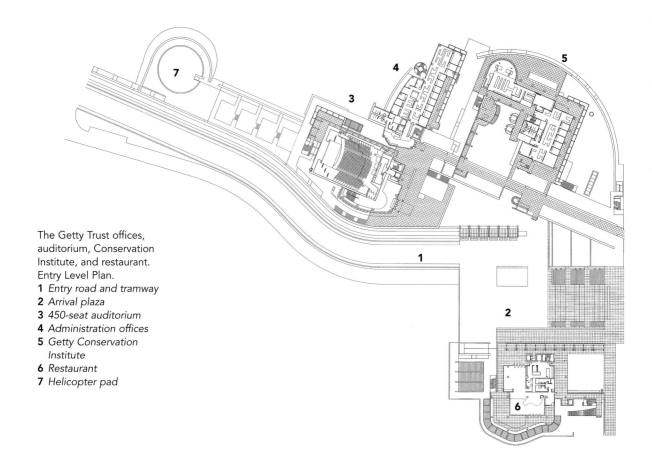

The Getty Trust offices, auditorium, Conservation Institute, and restaurant. Entry Level Plan.

1 *Entry road and tramway*
2 *Arrival plaza*
3 *450-seat auditorium*
4 *Administration offices*
5 *Getty Conservation Institute*
6 *Restaurant*
7 *Helicopter pad*

Changing Exhibitions

Concurrent exhibitions of varying sizes include rotating thematic installations as well as new acquisitions.

Wayfinding

Handheld CD-ROM players equipped with headphones are available in English and Spanish, helping visitors devise their own tours, offering overviews of galleries, and presenting interviews and commentaries by historians, artists, and conservators.

Education and Information

In the galleries, introductory wall texts provide context, and object labels indicate key points of each work. Gallery cards with additional information are located near gallery seating. In adjoining Art Information rooms, visitors may examine displays on manufacturing techniques, try hands-on activities, consult books, ask questions of staff, or use Art Access multimedia computer stations.

Family Room

Designed with children in mind, the family room is located prominently on the courtyard level. Here, staff members

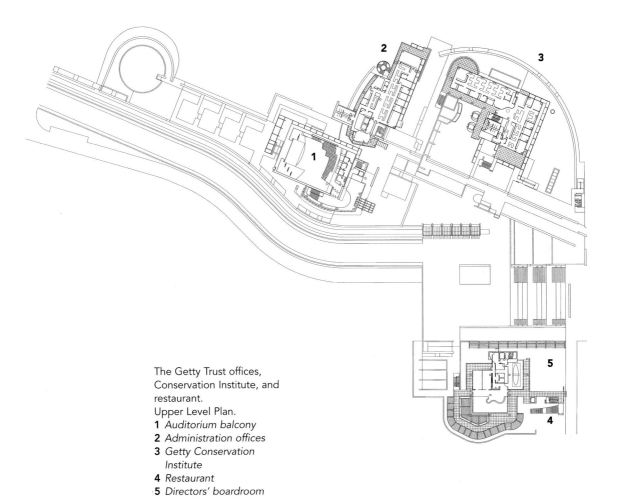

The Getty Trust offices,
Conservation Institute, and
restaurant.
Upper Level Plan.
1 *Auditorium balcony*
2 *Administration offices*
3 *Getty Conservation
   Institute*
4 *Restaurant*
5 *Directors' boardroom*

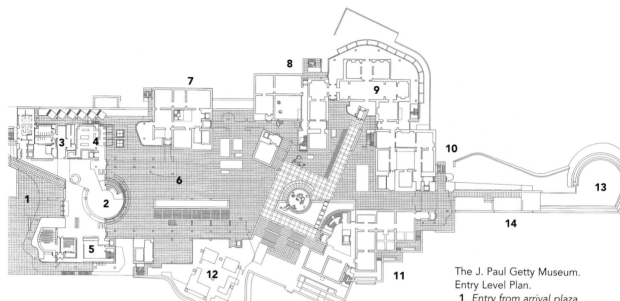

The J. Paul Getty Museum.
Entry Level Plan.
1 Entry from arrival plaza
2 Main lobby
3 Coat check and rest
    room
4 Bookstore
5 Orientation theaters
6 Museum courtyard
7 North art pavilion
8 East art pavilion
9 Decorative arts pavilion
10 South art pavilion
11 West art pavilion
12 Museum café
13 Gardens
14 South viewpoint

suggest resources such as game boxes, puzzles, books, and CD-ROMS, and give information on how to organize a visit. There is storytelling in the courtyard on weekends.

Food Service

The following facilities are included:

- Restaurant/café. A three-story building seating 650, located across the main plaza from the auditorium

- Cafeteria and full restaurant service on the two lower levels

- Private rooms for small groups and a large meeting room on the top floor

- Food and beverage carts in all open courtyards

- A café near the Special Exhibition Pavilion

Lighting

The design of the museum makes the most of natural light. Three pavilions have two-story atriums with stairs to both levels. Painting galleries have skylight systems that allow daylight to illuminate the pictures for as long as possible. A computerized system operates adjustable louvers regulated by sensors timed to the sun's movement.

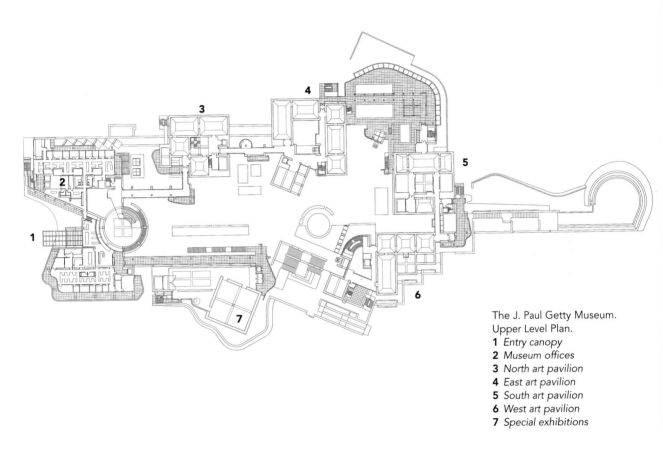

The J. Paul Getty Museum.
Upper Level Plan.
1 *Entry canopy*
2 *Museum offices*
3 *North art pavilion*
4 *East art pavilion*
5 *South art pavilion*
6 *West art pavilion*
7 *Special exhibitions*

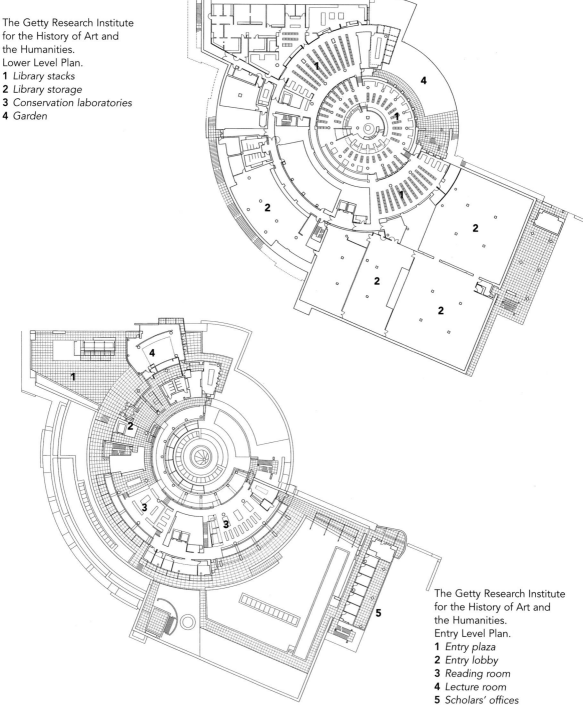

The Getty Research Institute
for the History of Art and
the Humanities.
Lower Level Plan.
1 *Library stacks*
2 *Library storage*
3 *Conservation laboratories*
4 *Garden*

The Getty Research Institute
for the History of Art and
the Humanities.
Entry Level Plan.
1 *Entry plaza*
2 *Entry lobby*
3 *Reading room*
4 *Lecture room*
5 *Scholars' offices*

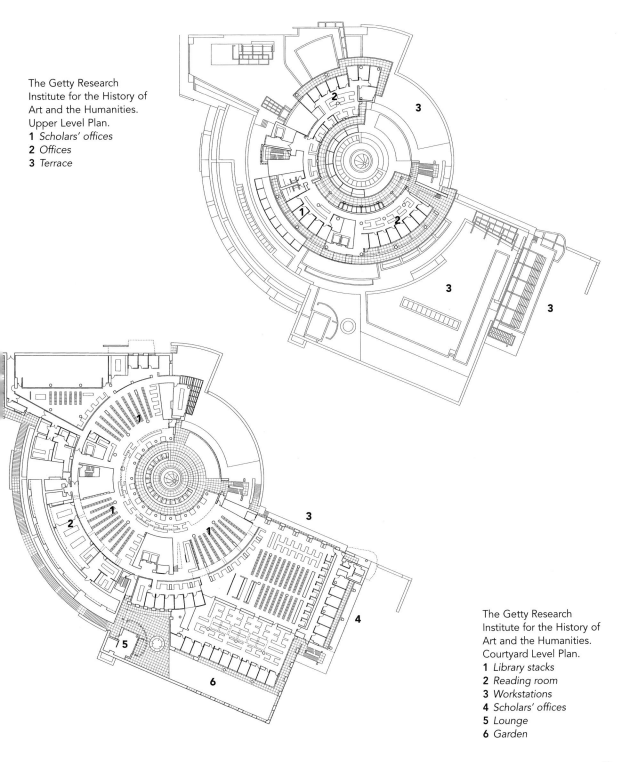

The Getty Research
Institute for the History of
Art and the Humanities.
Upper Level Plan.
1 *Scholars' offices*
2 *Offices*
3 *Terrace*

The Getty Research
Institute for the History of
Art and the Humanities.
Courtyard Level Plan.
1 *Library stacks*
2 *Reading room*
3 *Workstations*
4 *Scholars' offices*
5 *Lounge*
6 *Garden*

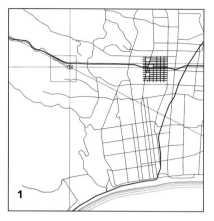 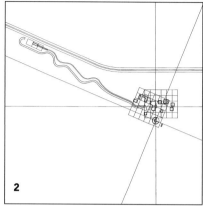 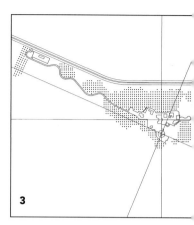

▲ Conceptual geometry of the Center in context.
1 *Within the city of Los Angeles*
2 *Basic geometry of the design concept*
3 *Landscape density surrounding the Center*
4 *Structural systems within the Center*
5 *Circulation systems within the Center*
6 *Major exterior spaces surrounding the Center*

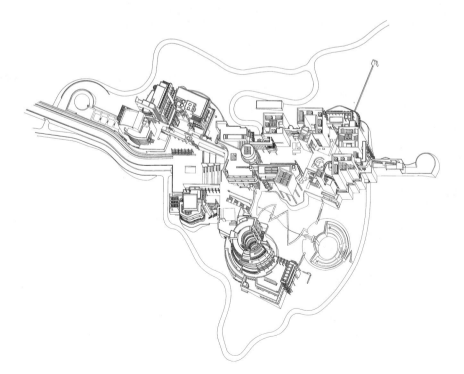

◀ Developed drawing illustrating the complexity and geometry of the Getty Center.

▶ Hilltop site plan.
1 *Auditorium*
2 *The Getty Information Institute and the J. Paul Getty Trust*
3 *The Getty Conservation Institute and the Getty Education Institute for the Arts*
4 *Tram station/arrival plaza*
5 *Restaurant and café*
6 *The J. Paul Getty Museum*
7 *The Getty Research Institute for the History of the Arts and Humanities*
8 *Central garden*

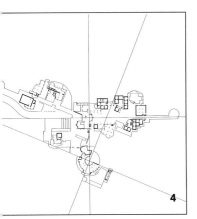

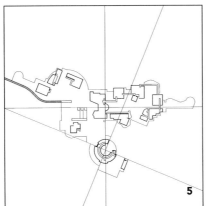

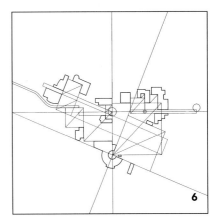

4

5

6

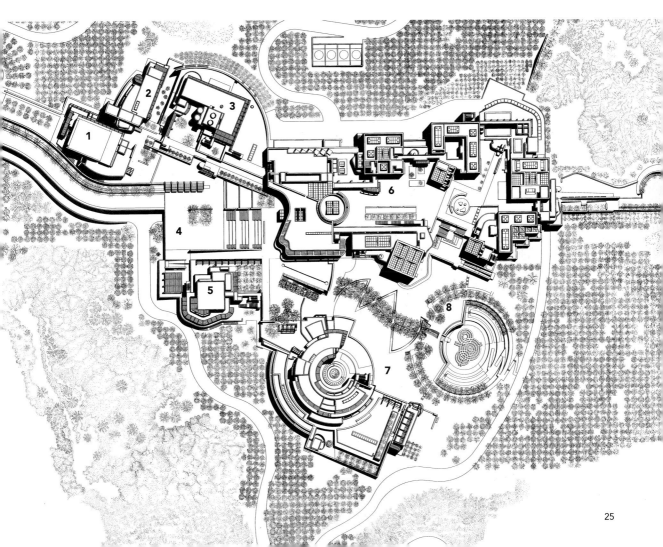

West elevation.

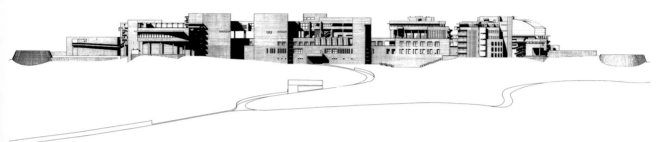

East elevation.

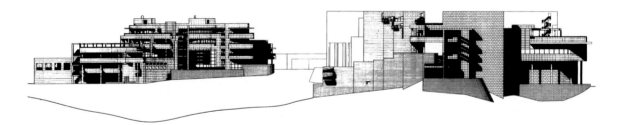

South elevation.

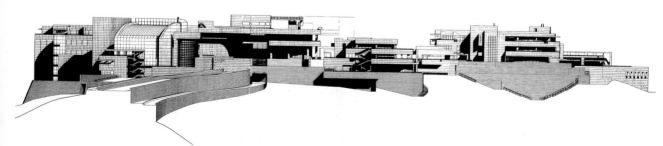

North elevation.

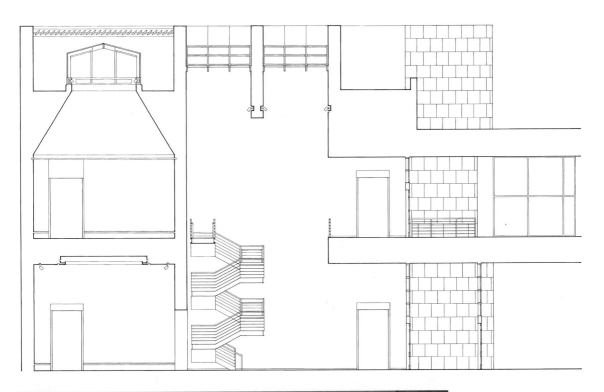

▲ Section through typical gallery and adjoining atrium. Note the gallery skylight and adjustable louvers above.

◀ View of Sculpture Gallery. Photo: Scott Frances/Esto

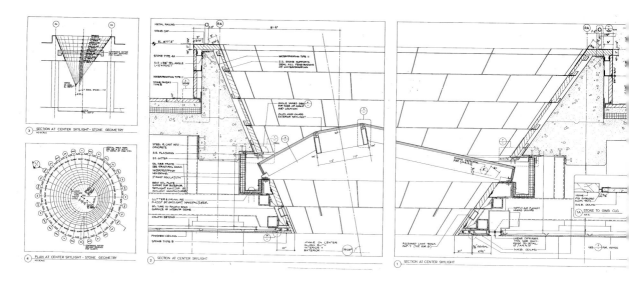

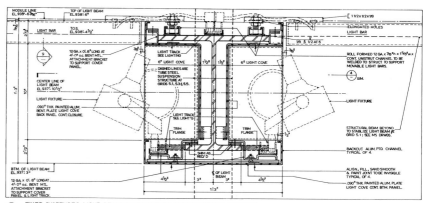

▲ Sections through center skylight at the Institute for the History of Art and the Humanities.

▶ Detail of fixed suspended light beam at Special Exhibition Gallery.

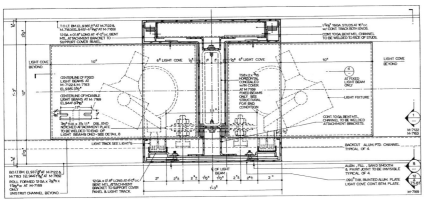

Detail of fixed and movable light beam at Special Exhibition Gallery.

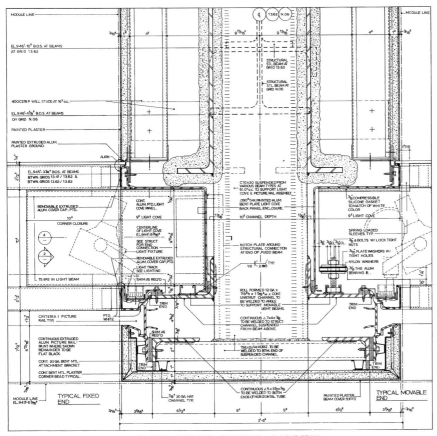

Detail of light cove and picture rail in Special Exhibition Gallery.

29

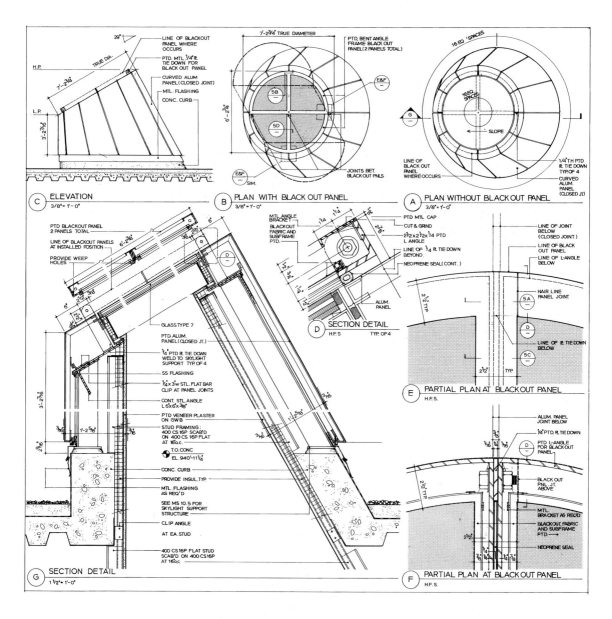

Section and detail of typical skylight. Note detail allowing placement of blackout panel to prevent light penetration.

View of Paintings Gallery.
Photo: Scott Frances/Esto

MIHO MUSEUM, *Shiga, Japan*
I. M. PEI, ARCHITECT (1997)

Background and Purpose

The religious order of Shinji Shumeikai is devoted to the pursuit of beauty in nature and in works of art, which the organization collects.

The Miho Museum combines both aims—nature and art—in an 82,865-sq-ft building, housing one of the world's finest ancient Japanese and early Western collections.

Site Planning

The museum building is related to its site and to nature, reflecting the religion of its sponsor. Its asymmetrical shape is determined by the contours of the site; its materials are derived from natural sources. The bulk of the building—nearly 80 percent—is recessed into the ground so that its wooded mountain setting remains substantially intact. For the same reason, and to avoid the scars of open-cut roads, approaches to the museum are negotiated around peaks and over valleys.

The site, selected by Kaishusama, spiritual leader of Shinji Shumeikai, is between twin ridges of a forest preserve, a mile from the sect's sacred precinct. But unlike that private sanctuary, the Miho is a public foundation with a projected public attendance of 70,000 annually.

Circulation

Visitors arrive from Kyoto by car or bus at a triangular reception pavilion housing a cafeteria and ticketing counter. To reach the museum, they are transported in small electric cars through one of two new tunnels cut into the mountains. Another service tunnel, 2,700 ft long, dedicated to art transport and emergency evacuation, curves around topographical depressions in order to remain underground and unseen.

After emerging from a tunnel 660 ft long onto a 400-ft suspension (or spiderweb) bridge spanning a precipitous drop, visitors are able to catch a glimpse of the museum in its undisturbed mountain paradise. There is little physical evidence of the building; it appears to be a series of skylights resting on the earth.

SIGNIFICANT ISSUES

Program
A museum for ancient Japanese and Western art

Circulation
Circuitous access to an isolated natural environment

Unique design concerns
Preservation of and harmony with an exceptional natural setting

Site planning
Shape and form of the building determined by contours of the site

Structure system
A sophisticated pedestrian footbridge leading to the museum's entrance

View of landscape from
center gallery between
North and South Wings.
Photo: Kiyohiko Higashide

1

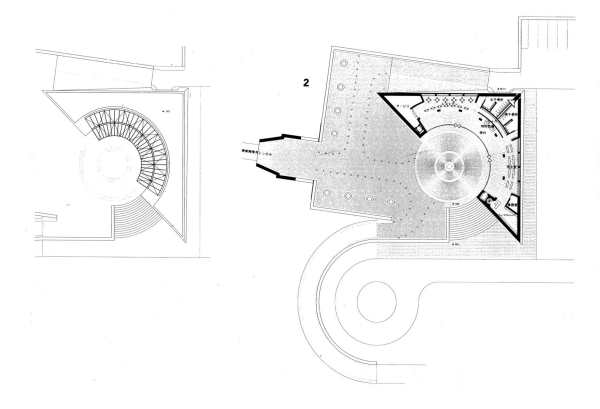

2

3

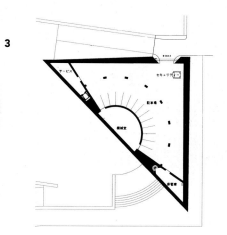

Plans of reception pavilion.
1 *Arrival platform*
2 *Cafeteria, ticketing, and shop*
3 *Service*

Plan.
1 *North wing: devoted to Japanese art, with Japanese garden open to sky*
2 *South wing: devoted to Western art, with administrative offices*
3 *Reception pavilion*

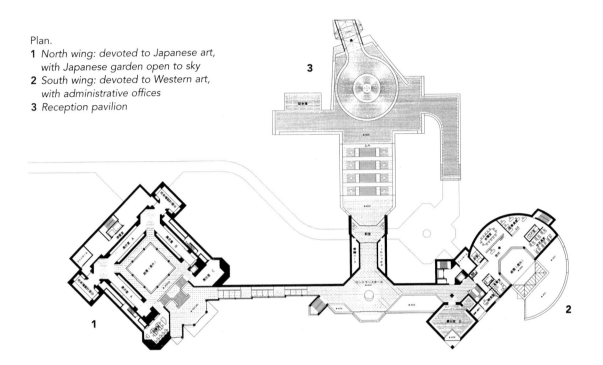

▲ Conceptual sketch by I. M. Pei.

◄ View from reception pavilion of suspension bridge and approch tunnel.
Photo: Kiyohiko Higashide

Visitors are let off at the museum's entry plaza. They then ascend a series of leveling terraces and enter the building's main public area, a metal space frame reception hall with a skylight and aluminum sunscreens. Through a transparent window wall, the reception hall views the valley sprawled to the west, overlooking a sacred precinct with a bell tower and sanctuary.

Design

From the reception hall, visitors proceed to the museum's north and south wings (each 10,750 sq ft).

The north wing is:

• Organized around a square Japanese garden left open to the sky

• Devoted to Japanese art

The curved south wing is:

• Three stories high

• Devoted to Western art

The top level of the south wing is occupied by administrative offices and Egyptian art galleries. Exhibition areas continue below with installations of Gandharan, Near Eastern, Greek and Roman, ancient Chinese, Sassanian, and Islamic art.

On the main level of the museum are located:

• An auditorium

• A public tearoom with an open courtyard

Housed below the main level are:

• Conservation laboratories

• Curatorial functions

• Storage and service facilities

Axonometric drawing.
1 *Reception pavilion*
2 *North wing: Japanese art*
3 *South wing: Western art*
4 *400-ft suspension bridge*

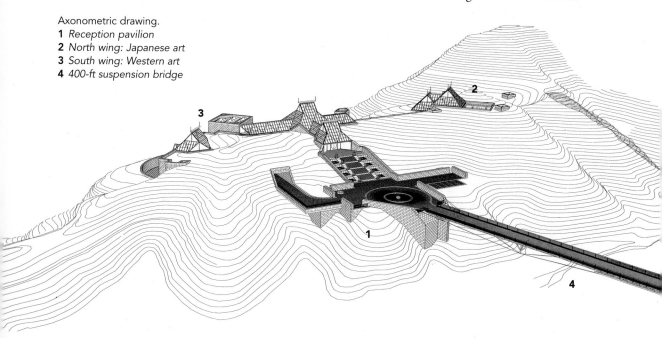

View of bridge and tunnel
approach.
Photo: Kiyohiko Higashide

View of Japanese garden in
north wing.
Photo: Kiyohiko Higashide

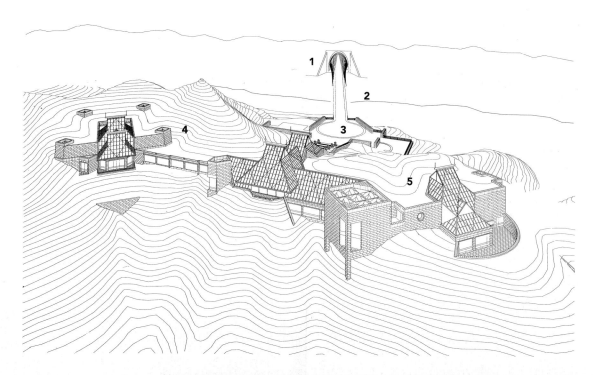

▲ Axonometric drawing.
1 *Tunnel approach*
2 *Suspension bridge*
3 *Reception Pavilion*
4 *North wing*
5 *South wing*

▶ Interior of south wing.
Photo: Kiyohiko Higashide

MUSEO DE ARTE DE PONCE, *Ponce, Puerto Rico*

EDWARD DURELL STONE, ORIGINAL ARCHITECT (1964)
RKK&G MUSEUM AND CULTURAL FACILITIES CONSULTANTS, MASTER PLAN ARCHITECTS (1998)

Background and Purpose

The Museo de Arte de Ponce was created and funded by Luis A. Ferré, a former elected governor of Puerto Rico. Its original design was International Style with a straightforward geometric plan.

Already an institution whose collections span several cultures and centuries, a comprehensive architectural plan—a master plan—is shaping its future as an art museum with goals beyond the interests of its own region. These goals are:

- Institutional (management and growth of the collections)

- Technological (preservation and safekeeping of the collections)

- Educational

New service entrance on Calle "A."

Site

The museum, with its view of the sea, is located near the center of Ponce in a historic area that contains some of the most important sites and buildings in Puerto Rico.

Its close proximity to the Catholic University of Puerto Rico and the College of Technology of the University of Puerto Rico suggests the possibility of joint exhibitions and other collaborative efforts.

Collections

The museum houses more than 3,000 works of art. Important among them are:

- Masterworks by José Campeche and Francisco Oller, major Puerto Rican artists
- Works by pre-Raphaelite painters Sir Edward Burne-Jones and Dante Gabriel Rossetti
- *Flaming June,* painted by Victorian artist Frederick Lord Leighton
- Collections of Puerto Rican graphic artists
- Puerto Rican folk art
- Latin American, Pre-Columbian, East Asian, and African art

Master Plan

The master plan would:

- Restore the existing building
- Upgrade interior spaces
- Integrate the old structure with the new

Main Floor

The main floor has these features:

- An airlock or enclosed vestibule at all existing entries to maintain constant

Area site plan.

SIGNIFICANT ISSUES

Program
A master plan for expansion and growth

Circulation
The integration of new and existing construction

Site planning
Using adjacent properties for expansion

Environmental challenges
Maintaining constant relative humidity in a tropical climate

Financing
Increasing income-producing opportunities

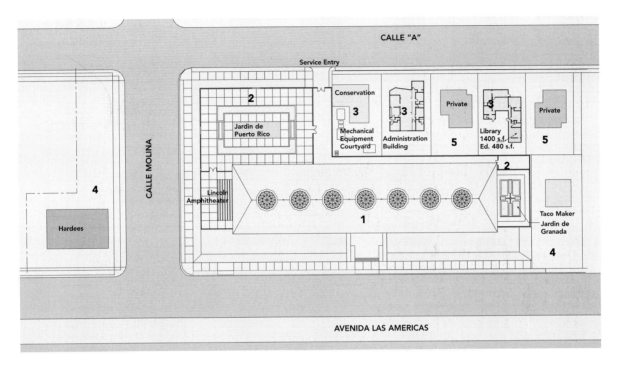

CALLE "A"

Service Entry

Conservation

3

Mechanical Equipment Courtyard

Administration Building

3

Private

Library 1400 s.f. Ed. 480 s.f.

Private

5

5

2

3

Jardin de Puerto Rico

CALLE MOLINA

4

Lincoln Amphitheater

1

2

Taco Maker

Jardin de Granada

4

Hardees

AVENIDA LAS AMERICAS

relative humidity and avoid dangerous radical fluctuations in humidity.

- A fully equipped loading dock and receiving entry with registrar's facility and security station, staff locker rooms, and passenger/freight elevator access to all floors, meeting requirements of the Americans with Disabilities Act (ADA).

- A café/restaurant and kitchen near the existing Jardin de Puerto Rico. The café will have independent access from the street and operate outside regular museum hours.

- A large central book/gift shop with merchandise storage and manager's office adjacent to the café/restaurant.

- A fully media-equipped 200-seat auditorium.

Second Floor

The second floor offers a number of features:

- Restoration of existing roofs and skylights, replacing them with recent advances in glazing materials that eliminate infrared (ultraviolet) penetration and control footcandle levels.

- Existing galleries refitted with energy-efficient and controlled-spectrum fixtures to ensure the safety of the artworks.

- The addition of administrative offices for the director, education director, curatorial staff, volunteers, and docents.

- A new library, including the museum catalog, study carrels, and an interactive computer center.

Existing site plan.
1 *Existing 1964 museum*
2 *Garden*
3 *Museum-use residential structures*
4 *Museum properties*
5 *Private properties*

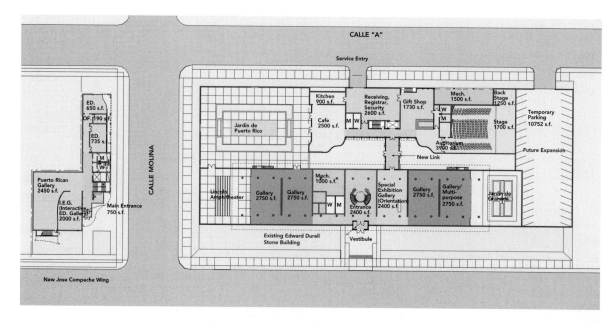

CALLE "A"

Service Entry

CALLE MOLINA

Kitchen
900 s.f.

Receiving,
Registrar,
Security
2600 s.f.

Gift Shop
1730 s.f.

Mech.
1500 s.f.

Back
Stage
1250 s.f.

Temporary
Parking
10752 s.f.

Cafe
2500 s.f.

M W

M

Stage
1700 s.f.

Jardin de
Puerto Rico

Auditorium
3900 s.f.

Future Expansion

New Link

ED.
650 s.f.

OF. 190 s.f.

ED.
735 s.f.

M
W

Puerto Rican
Gallery
2450 s.f.

Mech.
1000 s.f.

Gallery
2750 s.f.

Gallery
2750 s.f.

Special
Exhibition
Gallery
(Orientation)
2400 s.f.

Gallery
2750 s.f.

Gallery/
Multi-
purpose
2750 s.f.

Jardin de
Granada

I.E.G.
(Interactive
ED. Gallery)
2000 s.f.

Main Entrance
750 s.f.

Lincoln
Amphitheater

W M

Entrance
2400 s.f.

Existing Edward Durell
Stone Building

Vestibule

New Jose Compeche Wing

▲ Master plan/first floor.

▶ Existing museum on right,
with new wing on left.

View of new addition (*left*) and existing museum (*right*) from Jardin de Puerto Rico.

SPACE ANALYSIS

	Area (sq ft)
Existing Museo de Arte de Puerto Rico	32,000
New Construction:	
Circulation and common area	4,900
Library	2,000
Conservation and restoration	1,750
Receiving, registrar, security, general storage, loading dock	2,600
Administration	4,000
Café/food service	3,400
Auditorium (stage/backstage)	6,800
Education center	2,875
Puerto Rican gallery	2,500
Special exhibition gallery	5,000
Total	67,825

Penthouse Floor

This floor houses the art conservation and restoration departments, art storage, and mechanical/electrical spaces.

Calle Molina Site/The José Campeche Wing

This museum-owned property is the site of a two-story education center, special exhibition and Puerto Rican art galleries with the following facilities:

- Studio art classrooms
- Lecture rooms
- Outdoor studio art and children's play area
- Education center offices
- Adults' and children's rest-room facilities
- Special exhibition gallery
- Contemporary Puerto Rican art gallery

▲ View of completed museum from second-floor terrace.

▶ Model of complete master plan.

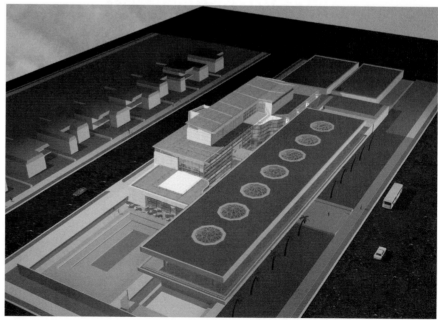

Income-Producing Sources

The new complex creates major opportunities for income-producing museum- and business-related special events. Setting the cultural institution architecturally free of its mercantile components by allowing them to function independently introduces a number of possible income sources that ultimately benefit the cultural institution.

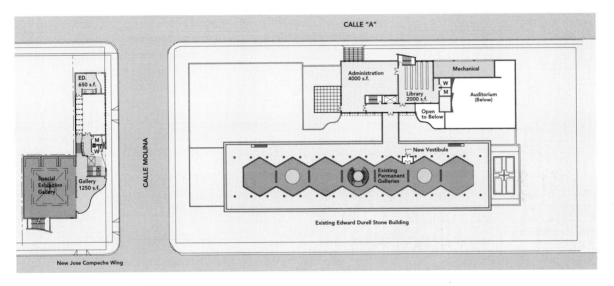

CALLE "A"

ED. 650 s.f.

Administration 4000 s.f.

Mechanical

Library 2000 s.f.

W
M

Auditorium (Below)

Open to Below

CALLE MOLINA

New Vestibule

Special Exhibition Gallery

Gallery 1250 s.f.

Existing Permanent Galleries

Existing Edward Durell Stone Building

New Jose Compeche Wing

▲ Master plan/second floor.

◄ View of José Compeche Education Wing.

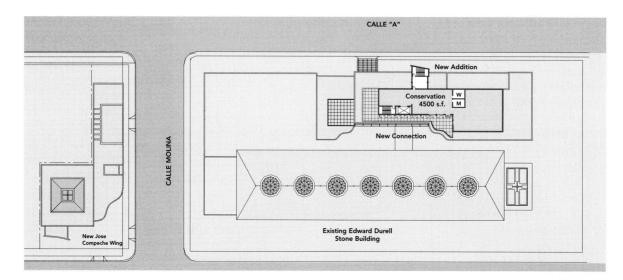

CALLE "A"

CALLE MOLINA

New Addition

Conservation
4500 s.f.

W
M

New Connection

Existing Edward Durell
Stone Building

New Jose
Compeche Wing

▲ Master plan/third floor, roof.

▶ Courtyard between new and existing wings.

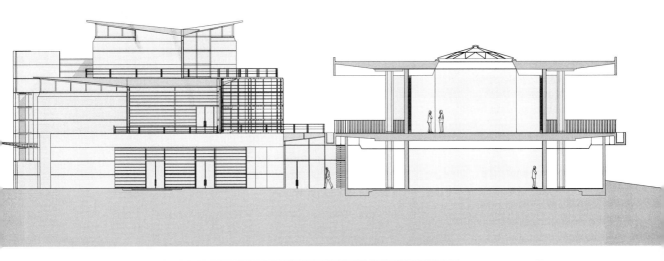

▲ North elevation.
Left: New wing
Right: Existing museum

◀ View from second floor of existing museum.

THE METROPOLITAN MUSEUM OF ART,
New York, New York
THE MASTER PLAN AND EXPANSION OF THE MUSEUM (1967–PRESENT)
KEVIN ROCHE JOHN DINKELOO AND ASSOCIATES, ARCHITECTS

The Metropolitan Museum of Art, founded in 1870, houses the largest collection of art in the United States and the fourth largest in the world—after the British Museum, Saint Petersburg's Hermitage, and the Louvre, in Paris.

Background and Site
Located within New York's Central Park, the museum's first entrances were inside the park. The park's designers, Frederick Law Olmsted, Calvert Vaux, and Jacob Wrey Mould, thought of the museum as a "building in the park." Vaux, in fact, was both a designer of the park and the architect for the museum's first building, completed in 1880.

With the completion of the Metropolitan's Great Hall by Richard Morris Hunt in 1903, the entry was moved to Fifth Avenue. Subsequent additions by McKim, Mead and White completed the Fifth Avenue façade and extended the museum farther into the park.

Master Planning
Long-term planning, or the development of a master plan, should be understood as a firm but flexible recommendation for the direction that a museum will take in completing its building. It is a guide for the future, a key to the logical and organic ordering of elements within a complex building type. Its challenges are many, combining political, social, historical, and financial ingredients with the passage of time and the ever-changing needs of the community to be served.

In 1967 Thomas Hoving, former Commissioner of Parks for the City of New York and curator of the Cloisters, the Metropolitan's Medieval Art Center in upper Manhattan, was named director of the museum. He initiated the Metropolitan's complete expansion and renovation that has taken more than 30 years to accomplish, at the same time respecting its historic landmark status and keeping unaffected sections of the museum open for normal use.

Master planning involved an extensive review of existing conditions and the development of a comprehensive plan for its completion.

Under consideration were the following:

- The state of existing collections

- The necessity to increase the display of important stored works of art

---

SIGNIFICANT ISSUES

Program
The most comprehensive program of museum expansion in history

Circulation
Bringing order to a century-old museum of more than 1 million sq ft

Unique design concerns
Restoration of and respect for historic wings by other architects

Site planning
The location of a building within a landmark park

Restored Fifth Avenue façade.

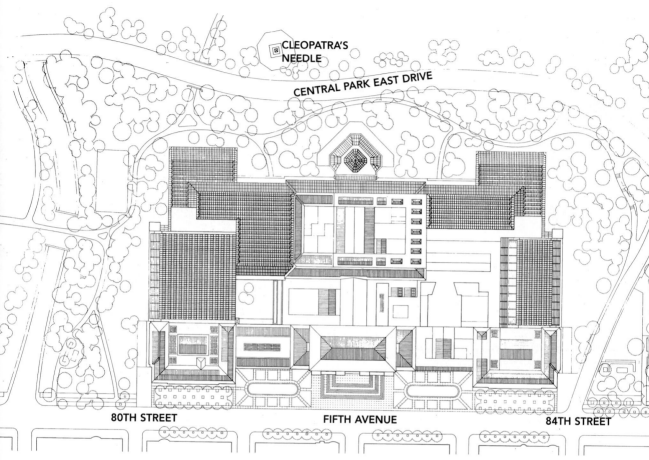

CLEOPATRA'S NEEDLE

CENTRAL PARK EAST DRIVE

80TH STREET   FIFTH AVENUE   84TH STREET

Site plan.

- The urgency to improve environmental standards for:
  Permanent and special exhibition galleries
  Art and general storerooms
  Administrative and curatorial offices
  Academic study centers
  Restoration, conservation, and scientific laboratories

- The need for circulation that would provide easy access for staff and visitors

The initial phase of the Master Plan was the redesign of the Fifth Avenue frontage of the museum to create an urban plaza with appropriately scaled, terraced steps leading to the restored Great Hall of 1903.

Rejecting the neoclassic style of the existing museum, the master plan architects, Kevin Roche John Dinkeloo and Associates, elected to introduce an architecture more like that which might be found in a park, such as for a greenhouse in a botanical garden. The resultant growth of the museum thus reflects a transition between the classical and garden/greenhouse architecture.

Restored Great Hall. Book and gift shops to the left; information counter in center.

New Galleries

A major need was for additional and larger galleries. Included among these were the following:

- The Sackler Wing for the Temple of Dendur and the Egyptian collections

- The Michael C. Rockefeller Wing for the arts of Africa, Oceania, and the Americas

- The Andre Meyer Galleries

- The American Wing, including restoration of architecture by Calvert Vaux, Louis Sullivan, and Frank Lloyd Wright

- The Lila Acheson Wallace Wing for modern art

The new additions maintain the high ceilings characteristic of the Metropolitan, and the proportions of the galleries vary according to the works displayed, often with carefully controlled natural light from extensive skylight sources.

Relief Spaces

The areas between the wings and the existing museum are left as skylighted courtyards, or relief spaces—the American Wing Garden Court (with the restored 1822 Assay Office Building façade) on the north, and on the south an "interior street" for European garden sculpture that preserves the restored 1888 façade by New York architect Theodore Weston. These relief spaces allow the visitor a chance to recover from the intensity of gallery viewing in an enormous and varied museum.

(text continues on page 58)

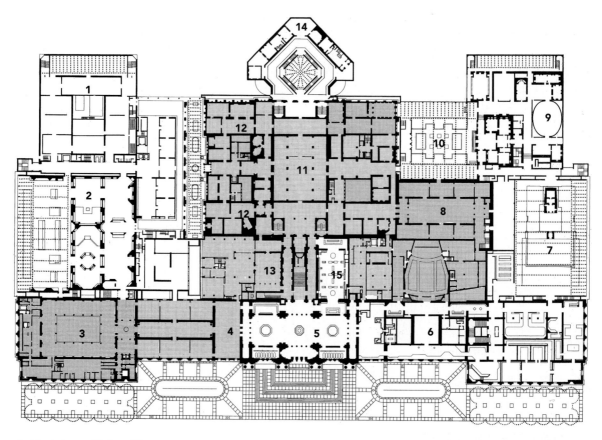

1 Lila Acheson Wallace Wing
  (twentieth-century art)
2 Rockefeller Wing (arts of Oceania,
  Africa, and the Americas)
3 Restaurant/café
4 Greek and Roman art
5 The Great Hall
6 Egyptian art
7 Temple of Dendur (Sackler Wing)
8 Arms and armor
9 The American Wing
10 American Wing courtyard
11 Medieval art
12 European sculpture and
   decorative arts
13 Library
14 Robert Lehman Wing
15 Retail shops

Far Eastern galleries.

Astor Chinese Garden.

Arts of Africa, Oceania, and the Americas (Michael C. Rockefeller Wing). Note vertical shades (*on left*) to control sunlight penetration.

▲ Exterior view of Lehman Wing. Virtually the entire building is underground.

▶ Twentieth-century art galleries. Note opaque ceiling panels to reduce natural light penetration from roof skylight.

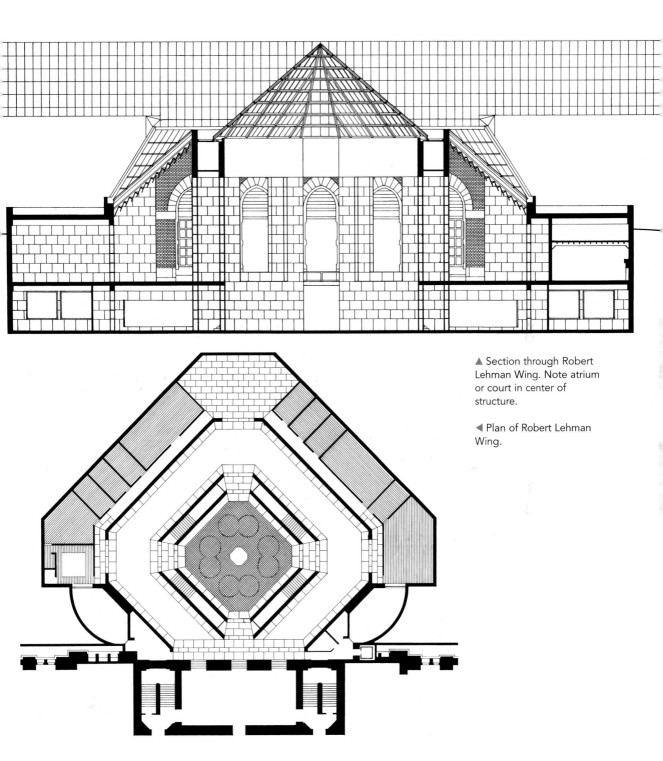

▲ Section through Robert Lehman Wing. Note atrium or court in center of structure.

◄ Plan of Robert Lehman Wing.

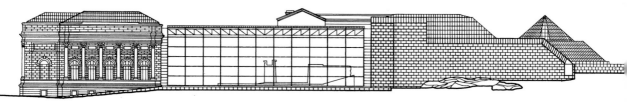

North elevation.

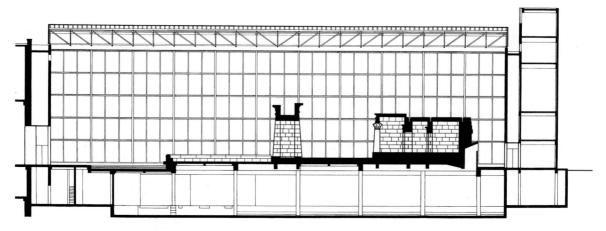

Section through Sackler Wing/Temple of Dendur. Completely enclosed in a glass structure, the reconstruction simulates the temple's original orientation on the Nile River in Egypt.

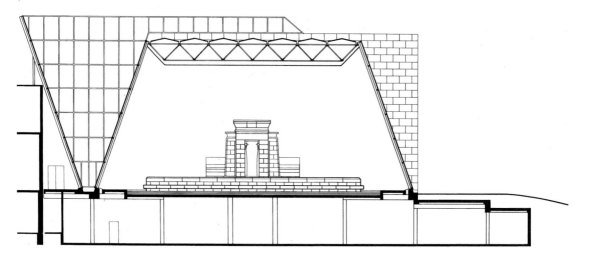

Section through Sackler Wing/Temple of Dendur. Service entrance is immediately below.

The Temple of Dendur
within the Sackler Wing.

Master Plan Projects

Master Plan projects designed by Kevin
Roche John Dinkeloo and Associates
include those listed in the table below.

SCOPE OF MASTER PLAN		
	Completion Date	Area (sq ft)
Fifth Avenue Plaza	1970	35,000
The Great Hall	1970	18,000
Bookshop	1970–1992	60,000
Robert Lehman Pavilion	1975	65,000
The Sackler Wing (Temple of Dendur)	1979	105,200
The American Wing	1980	175,000
Astor Chinese Garden Court	1980	5,300
Frank Lloyd Wright Francis Little House	1981	5,000
Michael C. Rockefeller Wing	1981	372,000
Andre Meyer Galleries	1981	12,000
Dillon Chinese Galleries	1981	7,700
Lila Acheson Wallace Galleries of Egyptian Art	1982	38,300
Uris Education Center	1982	31,000
Lila Acheson Wallace Wing for modern art	1986	126,000
The Japanese Galleries	1986	11,000
European Sculpture and Decorative Arts Wing	1988–1992	148,000
Weber Galleries for Art of Ancient China	1988	5,800
Florence and Herbert Irving Galleries for the Arts of South and Southeast Asia	1993	15,000
Greek and Roman Galleries	1999	15,000

European Sculpture Court. Note restored original Metropolitan Museum wing (Calvert Vaux, architect) on right.

Twentieth-century art galleries.

KIASMA MUSEUM FOR CONTEMPORARY ART,
Helsinki, Finland
STEVEN HOLL, ARCHITECT; JUHANI PALLASMAA, ASSOCIATE ARCHITECT (1998)

Background and Purpose
Commissioned by the Finnish Ministry of Education after an international competition, the Kiasma is the only museum of contemporary art in Finland.

It also serves as a forum for community events such as the following:

- Dance and music programs

- Seminars

- Poetry readings

- Roundtable discussions

Site
The building is located in central Helsinki, across from the parliament building and near Eliel Saarinen's

---

SIGNIFICANT ISSUES

Program
Creation of the only contemporary art museum in Finland, with facilities for the performing arts and community events

Unique design concerns
The relationship of the museum to nearby architecture

Site planning
A site with limitations

Lighting design
A building shape that allows wider distribution of natural light

Wayfinding
An entry atrium for independent access to museum spaces

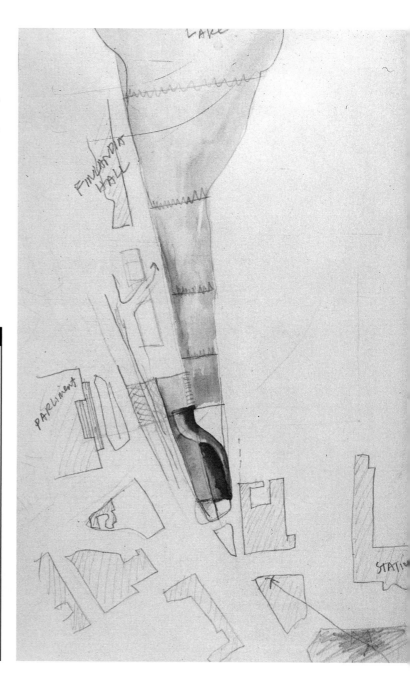

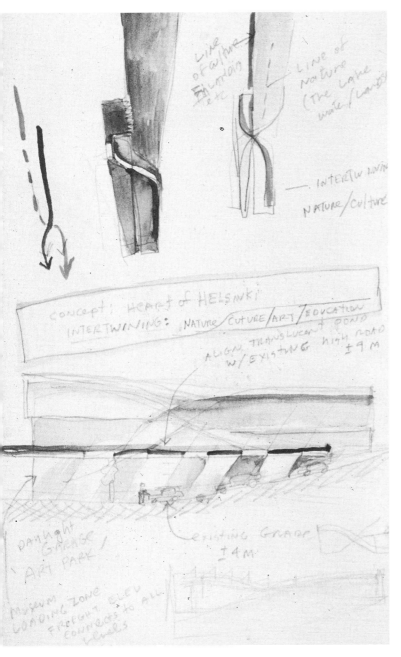

Helsinki Station and Alvar Aalto's Finlandia Hall Station. The shape and form of Holl's design relates to Finlandia Hall, Helsinki Station, and Helsinki's Toolo Bay.

Design

The museum consists of 38,700 sq ft of gallery space and 97,825 sq ft of service and support facilities.

The design is based on the concept of kiasma (or chiasma), a biological term for the intersection or crossing over of nerves or ligaments. Holl envisions the concept as the intertwining of the building's mass with the geometry of the city and the landscape.

The building is made up of two interlocking masses—a five-story curved structure and, within it, a smaller four-story rectangle containing:

• Galleries

• Offices

• A cafeteria

An entry atrium provides independent access to a ground-floor café, a bookshop, and a 240-seat auditorium/theater for film and video projection.

The 25 galleries are semirectangular, with one wall curved, allowing a flexible backdrop for the exhibition of art. Variations in gallery shapes and sizes are due to the gently curving section of the building.

Conceptual sketches by Steven Holl.

Kiasma

Site plan.

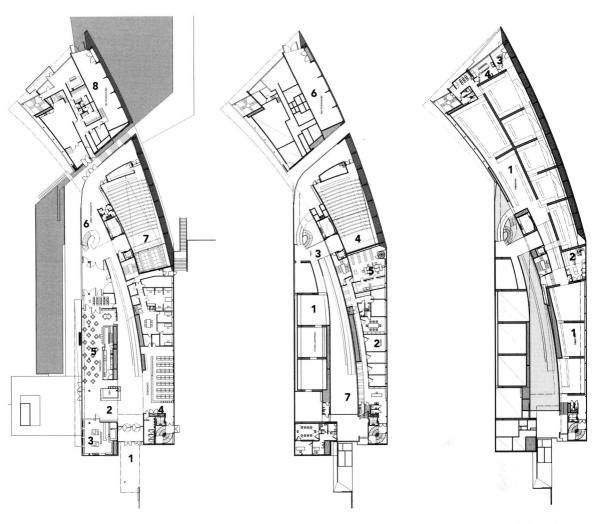

First floor plan.
1 Entry
2 Information
3 Bookstore
4 Coat check
5 Cafeteria
6 Auditorium lobby
7 Auditorium
8 Mechanical room

Second floor plan.
1 Permanent galleries
2 Offices
3 Lobby
4 Upper auditorium
5 Library
6 Mechanical room
7 Open to below

Third floor plan.
1 Galleries
2 Paper art
3 Lounge
4 Club room

Lighting

The museum's curvilinear shape plays an essential role in the distribution of natural light in Helsinki's northern latitude, where the sun never rises more than 51 degrees above the horizon.

The glazed western façade captures the sun's horizontal rays and deflects them through the central section to the

▲ Typical gallery with controlled natural light. Photo: Paul Warchol

▶ Fourth floor plan. Galleries.

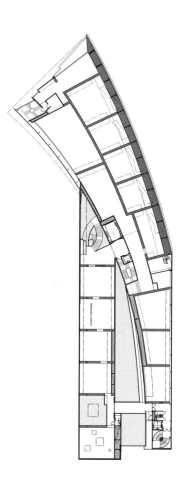

galleries below. Thus, natural light penetrates both upper and lower levels.

The curved roof section, with its "bowtie" skylights, introduces another means of distributing light to galleries below the top level. The building's intertwining form and the resulting interwoven torsion of space and light enable the galleries to be lighted naturally.

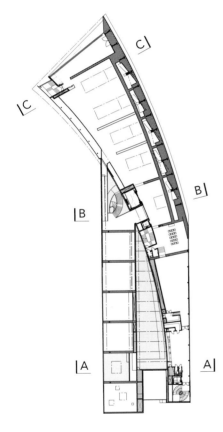

▲ View of typical upper gallery with controlled natural light source. Photo: Paul Warchol

◀ Fifth floor plan, key to sections.

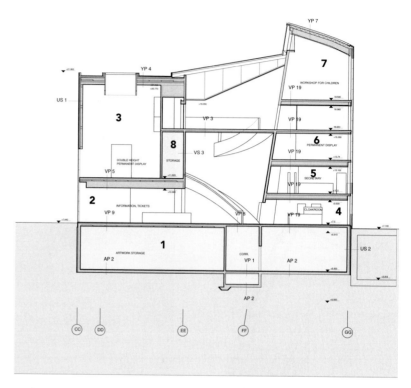

Section AA.
1 Art storage
2 Entry and information
3 Permanent galleries
4 Coatroom
5 Offices
6 Permanent galleries
7 Workshop for children
8 Storage

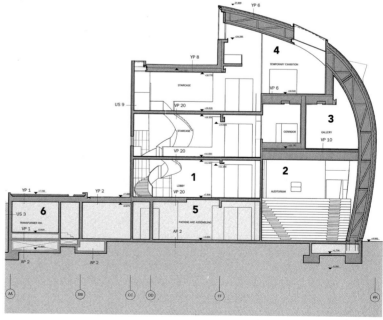

Section BB.
1 Lobby
2 Auditorium
3 Galleries
4 Temporary exhibitions
5 Packing and shipping
6 Transformer room

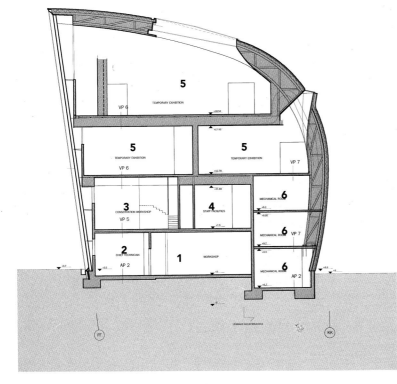

Section CC.
1 *Workshop*
2 *Chief technician*
3 *Conservator workshop*
4 *Staff facilities*
5 *Temporary exhibitions*
6 *Mechanical rooms*

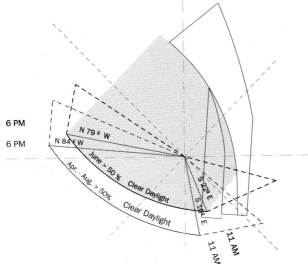

Sun-path reversal. Utilizing the unique properties of natural light in a latitude of 60 degrees north, the primary curvature of the building forms a reversal of the sun's path between 11:00 A.M. and 6:00 P.M., when the museum is open.

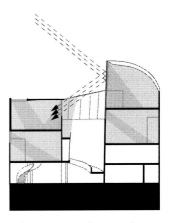

Light-catching section. The curved section captures the warm light of a horizontal sun, controlling and diffusing it through carefully oriented apertures to bring an optimum degree of natural light into the exhibition spaces.

SAINSBURY WING/NATIONAL GALLERY, *London, England*

VENTURI, SCOTT BROWN AND ASSOCIATES, ARCHITECTS (1991)

Purpose

Built on the last open space of London's Trafalgar Square, the Sainsbury Wing houses famous collections of early Italian and Northern Renaissance paintings.

Design

By means of a suspended walkway, the Wing is connected to and reflects the original National Gallery building, designed by William Wilkins in 1838, while maintaining its own identity as a work of contemporary architecture. It is faced with the same Portland limestone and observes the cornice height of the original.

Elements of the Wilkins façade are replicated on the new building, but used in innovative and unexpected ways alongside contrasting features—for example, large square-cut openings and small metal columns—to create a new rhythm and harmony.

Features of the new wing include the following:

- A new ground-level entrance, providing at-grade access to the entire combined National Gallery. This entrance is handicapped accessible, an important program consideration as museums reach out to growing and diverse audiences.

- A grand processional stair, visible through a large glass wall that overlooks the Wilkins building and Trafalgar Square. The stair leads from the lobby to third-floor permanent galleries displaying the Early Renaissance collection.

- Sixteen gallery rooms arranged in three parallel rows on the same level as the floors of the original National Gallery.

The sequence of old and new galleries creates an enfilade—the French system of aligning internal doors so that a vista is obtained through a series of rooms when all the doors are open. The enfilade was introduced in 1650 and became a feature of Baroque palace planning.

Lighting

The galleries are laid out in a gently implied hierarchy of small, medium, and large rooms, each lit by a delicately balanced and automatically controlled combination of natural and artificial light.

(text continues on page 74)

SIGNIFICANT ISSUES

Program
An addition to London's National Gallery to house the world's finest collection of Early Renaissance art

Unique design concerns
A contemporary structure combined with a historic museum and site

Lighting design
Automatically controlled light louvers

Wayfinding
Introduction of enfilade, a form of visual orientation

Financing
A public institution with private financing

View of Sainsbury Wing of
the National Gallery on
Trafalgar Square, London.
Photo: Matt Wargo

ART MUSEUMS

Basement plan.
A *Temporary exhibition galleries*
B *Lecture theater*
C *Cinema*

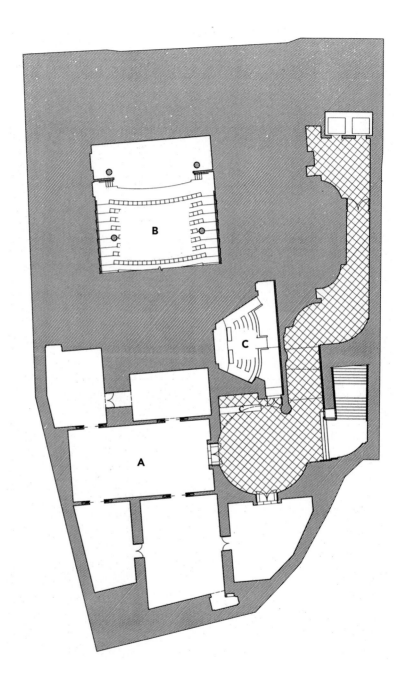

Lower ground floor.
A *Lecture theater*
B *Temporary exhibition
galleries below*
C *Gallery foyer below*
D *Projection booth*

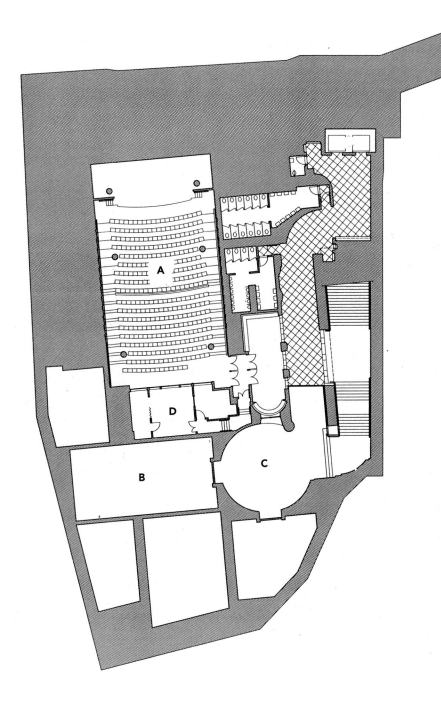

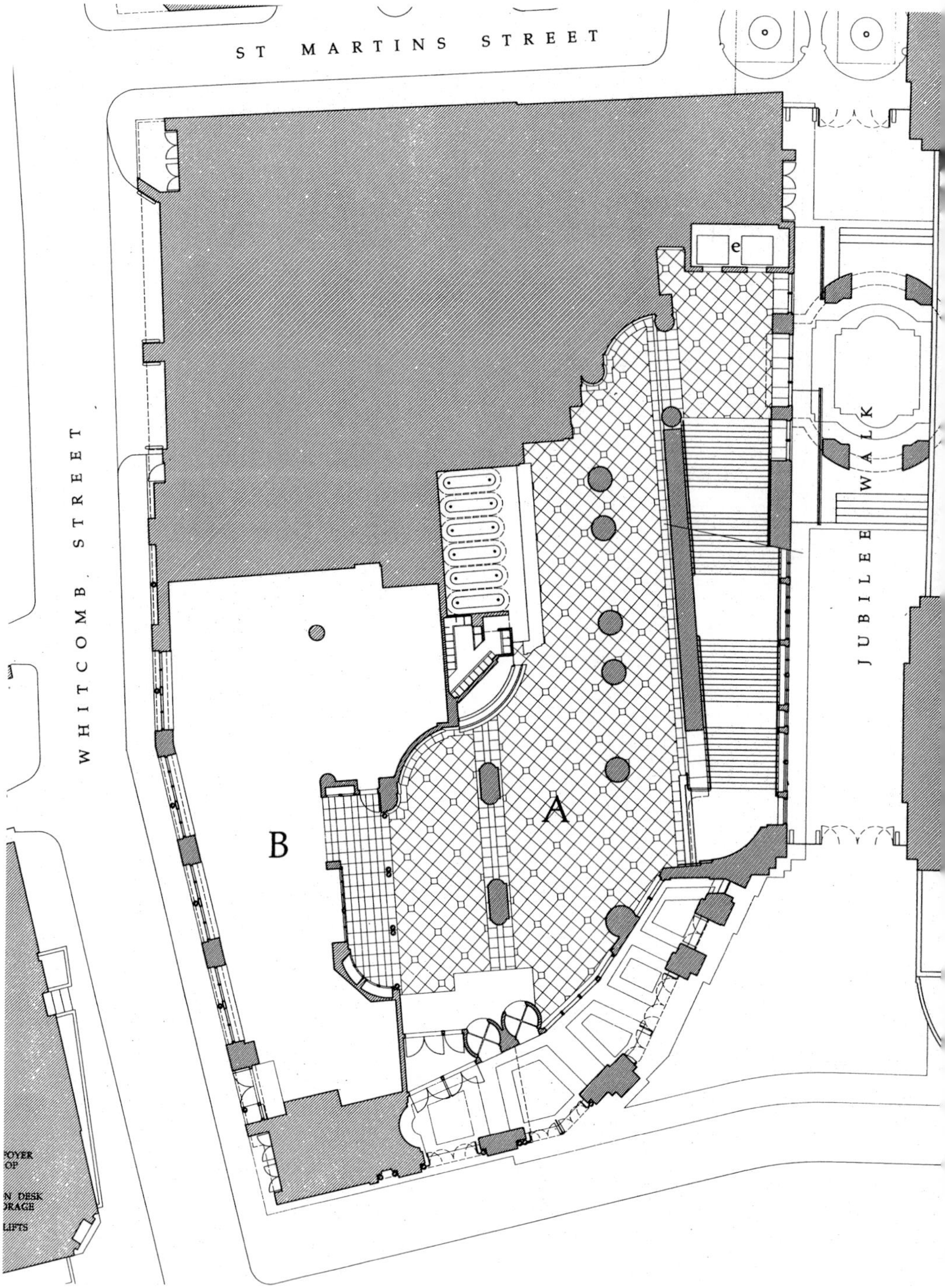

Ground floor.
A *Entrance foyer*
B *Gallery shop*

ST MARTINS STREET

WHITCOMB STREET

JUBILEE WALK

B

A

e

FOYER
OP

N DESK
ORAGE

LIFTS

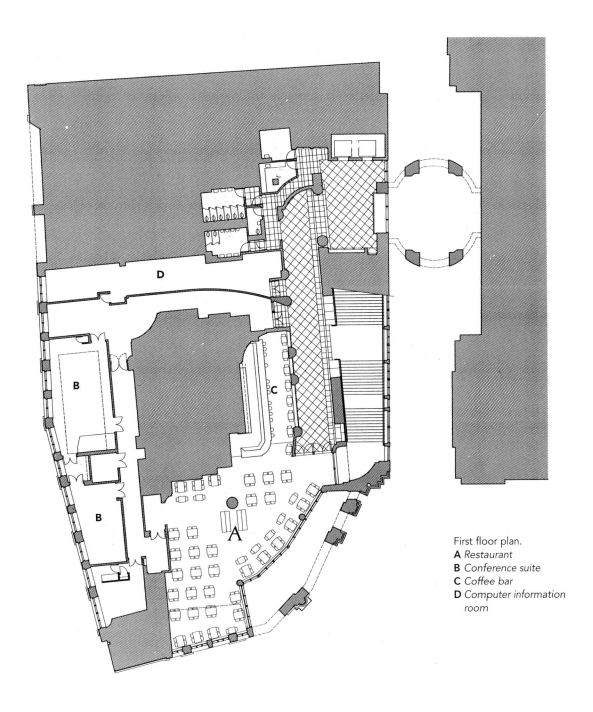

A

First floor plan.
A *Restaurant*
B *Conference suite*
C *Coffee bar*
D *Computer information
  room*

Clerestories, or windowed walls, with an elaborate system of sensor-operated louvers, allow filtered (nonultraviolet) natural light into each gallery space for optimal viewing conditions and energy efficiency. Through the clerestories, one is also made aware of the changing light outside.

The gallery ceiling lunettes (semicircular openings), coves, and lanterns (small, circular or polygonal turrets with windows all around) recall Sir John Soane's Dulwich College Picture Gallery (Dulwich, England, 1814).

This basic arrangement, a sequence of connected rooms, top-lit to leave large areas of blank wall for the display of pictures, has become a model followed by many art gallery architects.

Wayfinding

Some galleries contain windows that overlook other interior spaces or offer glimpses of the outside, offering light and helping visitors to orient themselves within the building.

A grand processional stair and public elevators combine to provide visual access to galleries and public facilities such as:

- Conference rooms

- A restaurant

- A 350-seat lecture theater

- An enlarged museum book/gift shop

- An interactive information center

Finance

An international competition and the completed project were entirely financed by private funds.

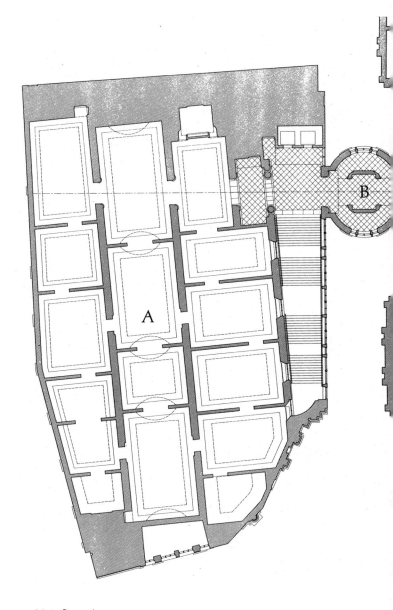

Main floor plan.
A *Early Renaissance and Northern European galleries*
B *Bridge to existing galleries*

Renaissance and Northern European galleries. Note abundance of controlled natural light.
Photo: Phil Starling

Entrance foyer and information center. Gallery shop in the distance on the left.
Photo: Phil Starling

Renaissance and Northern European galleries.
Photo: Phil Starling

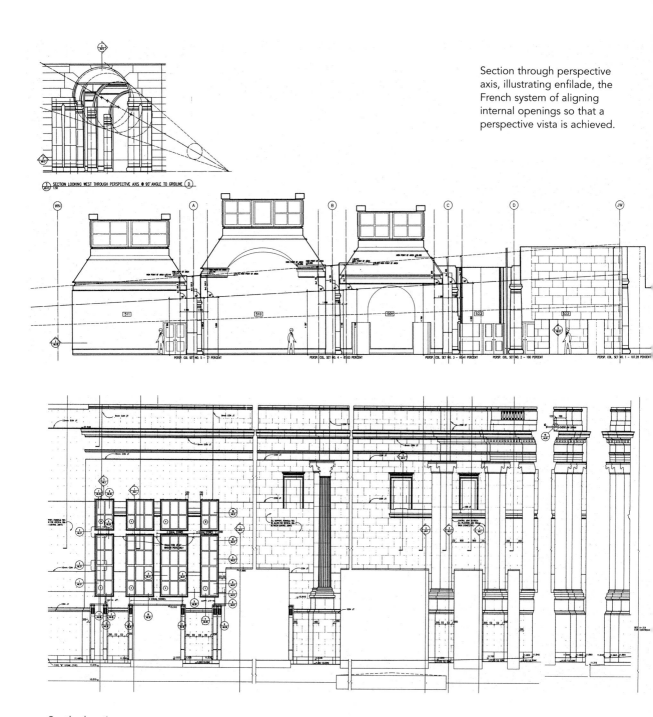

Section through perspective axis, illustrating enfilade, the French system of aligning internal openings so that a perspective vista is achieved.

South elevation.

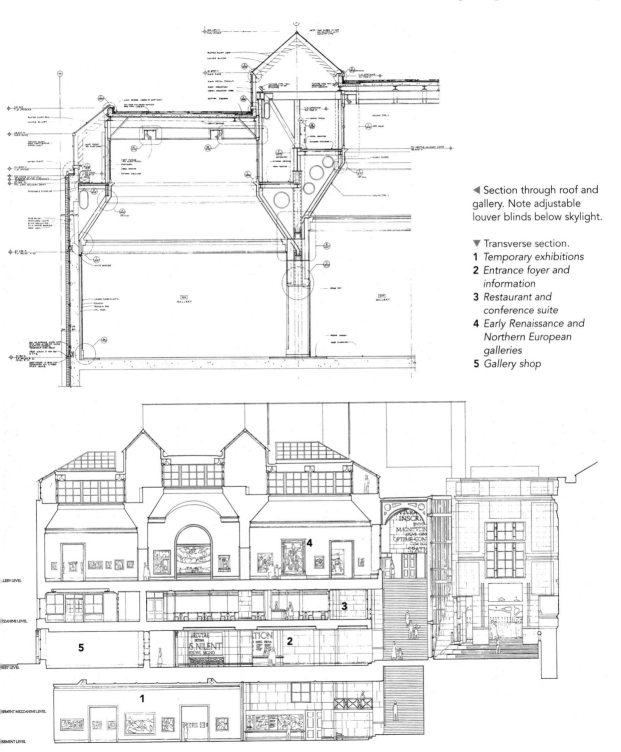

◄ Section through roof and gallery. Note adjustable louver blinds below skylight.

▼ Transverse section.
1 *Temporary exhibitions*
2 *Entrance foyer and information*
3 *Restaurant and conference suite*
4 *Early Renaissance and Northern European galleries*
5 *Gallery shop*

ARTHUR M. SACKLER MUSEUM, *Harvard University, Cambridge, Massachusetts*

JAMES STIRLING MICHAEL WILFORD & ASSOCIATES, ARCHITECTS (1985)

Purpose

The Stirling-Wilford addition to the Harvard University art museums (primarily the Fogg Art Museum) adds more than 61,000 sq ft (or 75 percent) of total gallery area. It doubles the number of classrooms and faculty office space. It also houses:

- Ancient, Asian, and Islamic art
- Special exhibition galleries
- Curatorial and service departments
- Library collections

The transfer of collections, departments, and offices to the new building freed space in the Fogg for the exhibition of the university's permanent collection of European and American art, most of which was in storage.

SIGNIFICANT ISSUES

Program
Expansion of a legendary university museum, providing essential support services

Circulation
An addition on a separate site poses special problems

Unique design concerns
An overtly modern building on a campus noted for its traditional architecture

Lighting design
Innovative skylights control and maintain acceptable levels of natural light

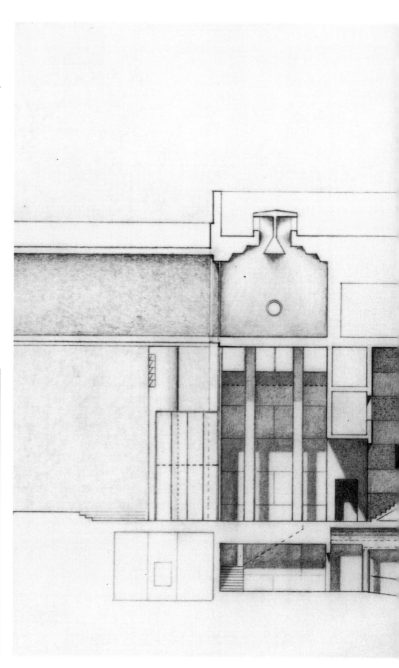

Long section through entrance
hall and central staircase.

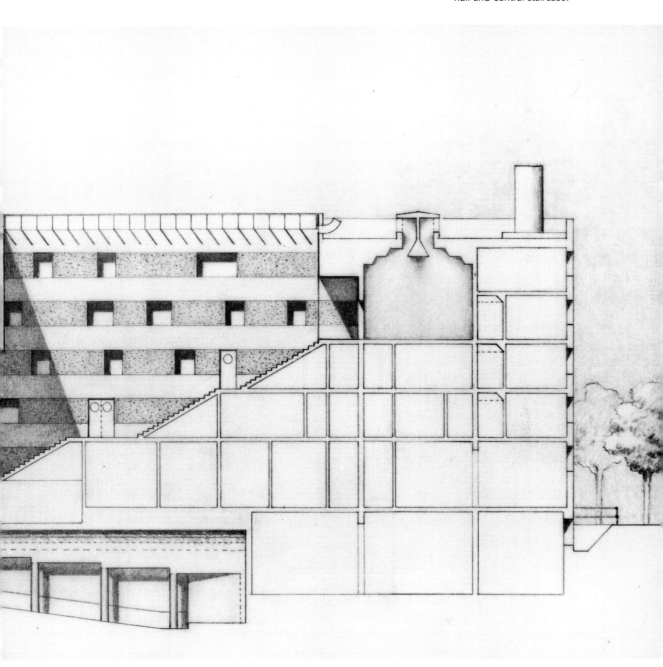

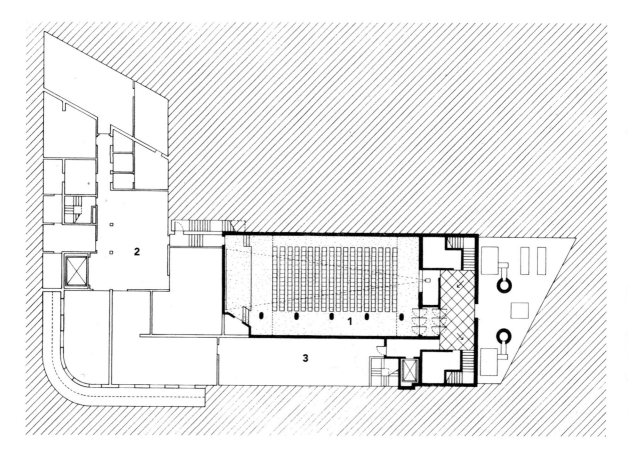

Basement level 1 plan.
1 *Lecture theater*
2 *Maintenance and operations*
3 *Storage*

Other departments that have expanded into vacated space in the original building include the following:

- A center for conservation

- The Department of Prints, Drawings, and Photographs

- The Fine Arts Library

Circulation

Visitors to the Sackler enter from Broadway into a formal entrance hall. Stairs at either side lead to a 300-seat lecture hall on the lower level, used for university teaching and for museum-sponsored public events. A Stirling signature skylight staircase rises through the center of the building to all gallery levels. To the left of the stair are five office levels; to the right are three levels of public galleries.

Collections

Gallery space for collections comprises the following:

- Special exhibitions (2,700 sq ft)

- Arab, Persian and Indian miniatures, textiles, and decorative arts (760 sq ft)

- Chinese and Japanese paintings, ceramics, and other decorative objects (1,792 sq ft)

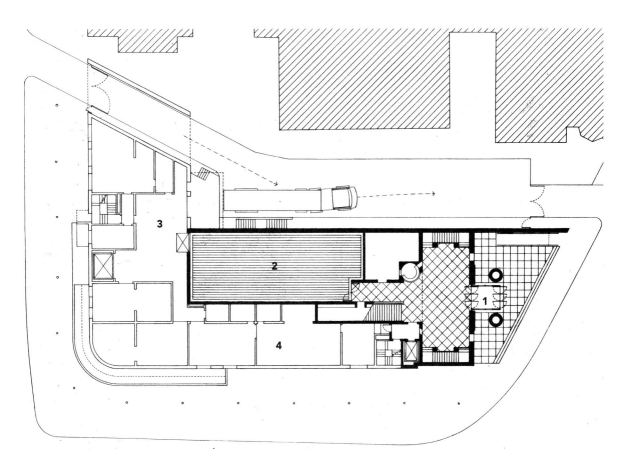

- Japanese prints (617 sq ft)

- Early Chinese art of the Shang through the Han dynasties (1,125 sq ft)

- Paintings from the Tun-huang caves and reliefs from the Tien-lung-shan caves (629 sq ft)

- Buddhist art, Chinese and Japanese sculpture (643 sq ft)

- Indian and Cambodian sculpture (585 sq ft)

- Art from Egypt and the Ancient Near East (452 sq ft)

In addition to:

- Four galleries of Islamic, Chinese and Japanese art (primarily delicate objects on paper and silk)

- The Roman Gallery (large sculptures, portrait busts)

Lighting

On the third, or uppermost, gallery level, natural lighting is introduced through a specially designed series of ceiling baffles that control:

- Ultraviolet portions of the spectrum

- Footcandle levels

Entrance level 1 plan.
1 *Entrance*
2 *Ground-floor gallery*
3 *Service entrance*
4 *Administration*

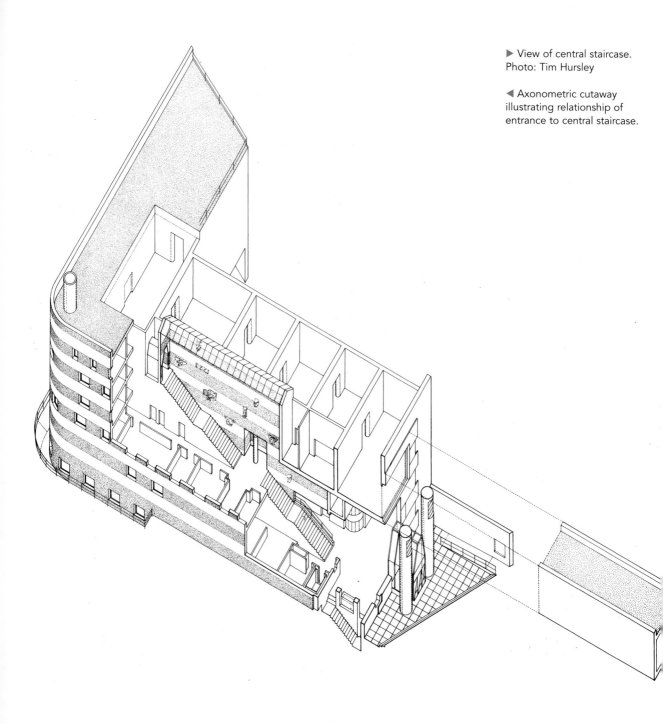

▶ View of central staircase.
Photo: Tim Hursley

◀ Axonometric cutaway
illustrating relationship of
entrance to central staircase.

Support Facilities

Support facilities at the Sackler include the following.

- Lower level:
  Expanded capabilities for mounting exhibitions
  Storage and mechanical areas
  Photography studios
  Offices and workrooms for the museum registrar

- First (street) floor:
  Shipping and receiving facilities
  Loading dock

- Second office level:
  Museum publications editor
  Membership department
  Public relations and press
  Additional curatorial offices
  Study room and storage areas for the Asian art department

- Third office level:
  Departments of Ancient Art, Asian Art, and Islamic and later Indian Art
  Faculty offices
  Seminar room

- Fourth office level:
  Curatorial offices
  Seminar room
  Storage areas
  Facilities for the Aga Khan Program for Islamic Studies

- Fifth office level:
  The Rubel Asiatic Research Library of the Harvard Fine Arts Library

SCHEDULE OF PROGRAM AREAS

	Area (sq ft)
Permanent galleries	8,610
Changing (temporary) galleries	2,600
Study Collection galleries	3,100
Lecture auditorium	2,650
Reading room and library	1,020
Offices and backup facilities	41,795
Entrance and circulation	1,225
Total Area	61,000

ART MUSEUMS

Exterior view of main
entrance.
Photo: Tim Hursley

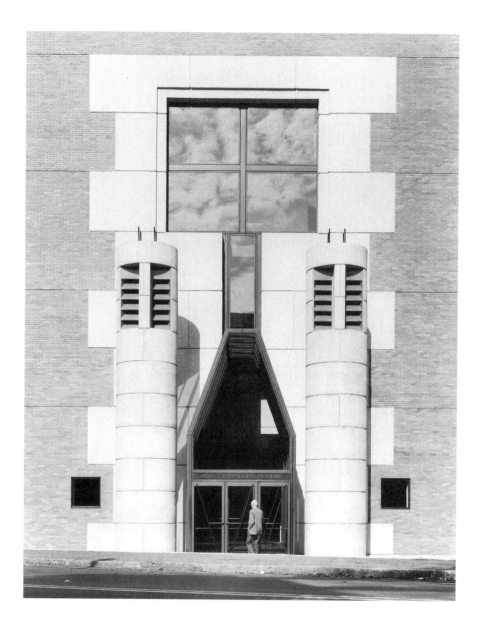

Interior of main entrance.
Photo: Tim Hursley

▲ View of typical gallery.
Photo: Tim Hursley

▶ First gallery level.
1 *Galleries*
2 *Administration and curatorial*

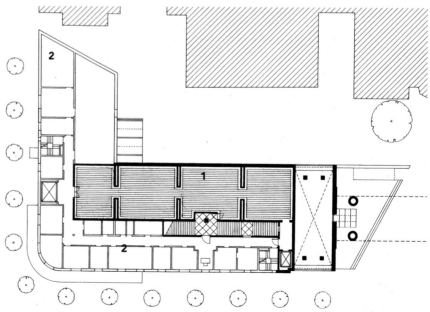

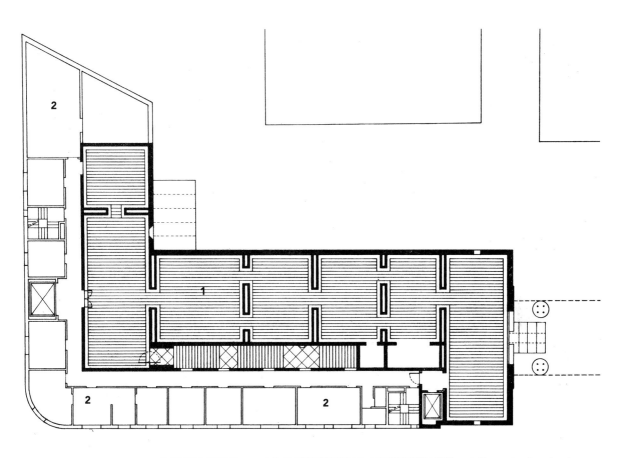

▲ Second gallery level.
1 *Galleries*
2 *Administration and curatorial*

◄ View of second gallery level (top gallery with skylight).
Photo: Tim Hursley

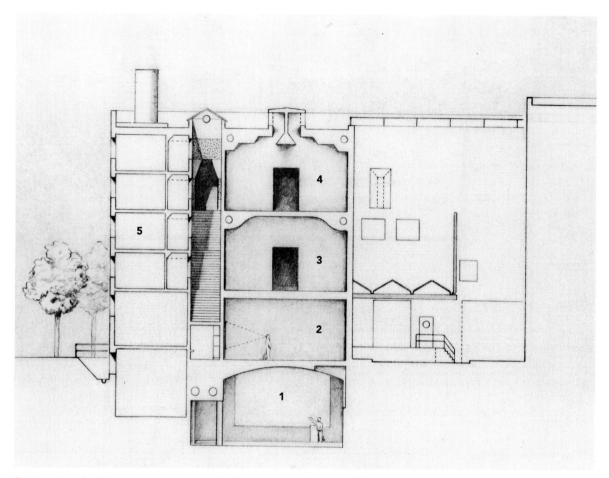

Cross section showing
offices, central staircase,
galleries, and basement
lecture theater.
1 *Lecture theater*
2 *Entrance level*
3 *First gallery level*
4 *Second gallery level*
5 *Administration and
curatorial*

FRYE ART MUSEUM, *Seattle, Washington*

PAUL THIRY, ORIGINAL ARCHITECT (1952)
OLSON SUNDBERG, ARCHITECTS (1999)

Background and Purpose

In 1888, Charles and Emma Frye moved to Seattle's First Hill District and filled their house with paintings they had purchased on trips to Europe. To preserve the collection, Frye specified in his will conditions to allow for the creation of an art museum for the people of Seattle.

According to the bequest, there must be:

- Three galleries, each 30 ft by 60 ft

- Display of all artwork on a single floor

- A significant daylighting component in all galleries

SIGNIFICANT ISSUES

Program
Expansion and reconstruction of an eclectic structure

Unique design concerns
Need for strict conformance to the donor's will

Lighting design
Particular use of natural light in galleries

Renovation
Careful demolition offers design opportunities

Entrance to the Frye Art Museum.

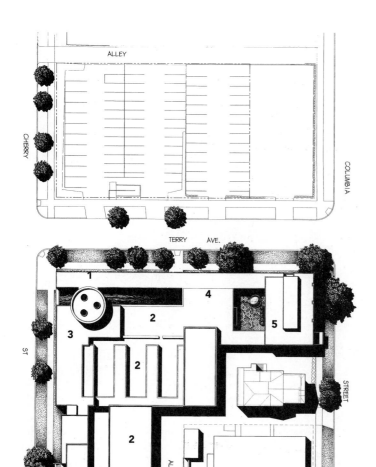

Site plan.
1 Entrance rotunda
2 Galleries
3 Museum store
4 Gallery café
5 Education wing
6 Service wing

The original Frye Museum, designed in unadorned International Style, opened near downtown Seattle 12 years after Charles Frye's death.

Two small additions followed— exhibit galleries and back-of-house support spaces. In 1984 a new entrance was designed.

In 1995 the firm of Olson Sundberg was hired to recreate the original museum while maintaining the integrity of the Frye will.

Program

The new program required:

- The eclectic assemblage of earlier changes and renovations by diverse architects into a cohesive whole

- Daylight in all galleries, while also meeting contemporary standards for art preservation

- Creation of:
  A studio art building
  A café
  An auditorium
  A museum shop
  Additional curatorial and
    administrative offices
  Back-of-house support facilities.

- State-of-the-art design, following museum standards set by the American Association of Museums*

---

*For information, write: American Association of Museums, Committee on Accreditation, 1575 Eye Street NW, Washington DC 20005; tel: 202-289-1818.

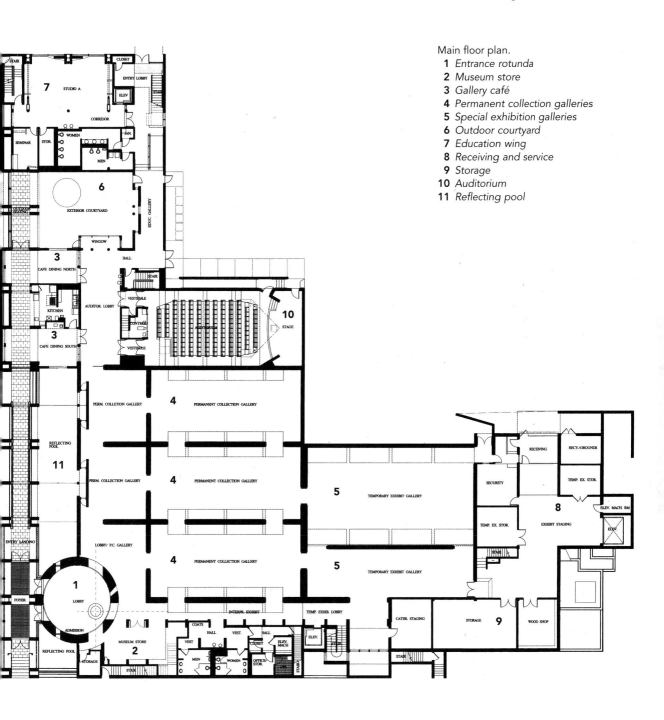

Main floor plan.
1 Entrance rotunda
2 Museum store
3 Gallery café
4 Permanent collection galleries
5 Special exhibition galleries
6 Outdoor courtyard
7 Education wing
8 Receiving and service
9 Storage
10 Auditorium
11 Reflecting pool

▼ Second floor plan
1 Administration and
  curatorial
2 Education wing, studios
3 Art storage

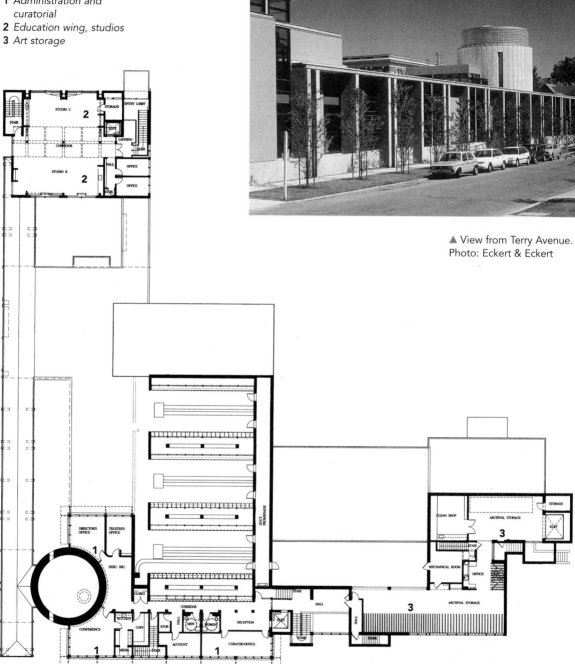

▲ View from Terry Avenue.
Photo: Eckert & Eckert

Design and Lighting

Problem

- In this latitude, on an overcast day solar brightness may exceed 2,000 footcandles. Museum curators would permit no more than a total of 24 footcandles on paintings and 8 footcandles on works of art on paper or other organic materials.

Some Solutions

- In the west galleries, walls that allowed light to bounce off the exterior reflecting pool into the interior spaces were recessed. Thus, natural light enters the gallery indirectly, not shining on areas displaying works of art.

- In the permanent galleries (Paul Thiry's original structure) new tall, vertically proportioned walls were added to take advantage of earlier clerestory-like natural light sources. Here again, daylight washes down the walls without touching the art.

The design process included the following:

- Building large-scale color models of portions of the building

- Hiring a lighting consultant to reproduce in a laboratory the sun angles and sky conditions of the region around the museum

- Using the models to test footcandle readings within the museum itself

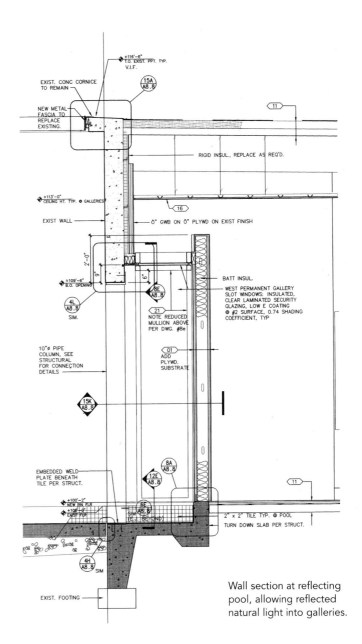

Wall section at reflecting pool, allowing reflected natural light into galleries.

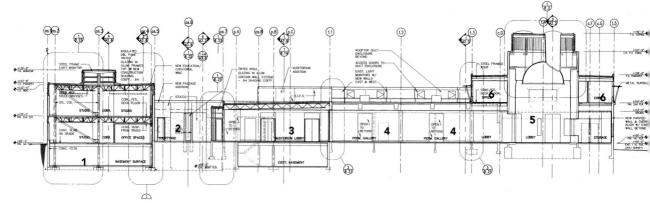

▲ Section through education wing, offices, entrance rotunda and galleries.

1 *Education wing*
2 *Open courtyard*
3 *Auditorium lobby*
4 *Galleries*
5 *Entrance rotunda*
6 *Offices*

▶ Entrance rotunda with information desk. Gift shop is in the distance.

Rendered section of entrance rotunda.

Careful demolition led to design opportunities:

- During remodeling, a skylight was revealed, and the structural beauty of its concrete cantilevered components exposed.

- An entrance rotunda was newly constucted, allowing additional daylight to enter through the resultant oculus.

- The ceilings were raised, bringing in more daylight.

Without violating any of the provisions of Frye's will, the architects gave the museum new life and new light. Today, the Frye has 42,000 sq ft of renovated and expanded space.

Rendered section through
galleries.

▲ Studio art classroom in education wing.

◀ Two views of permanent exhibition galleries.

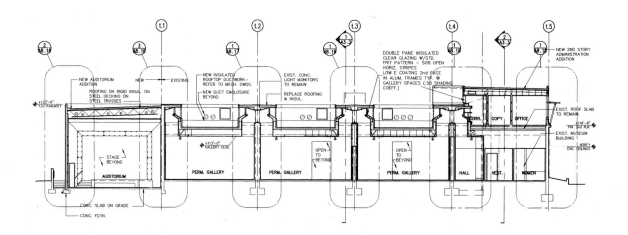

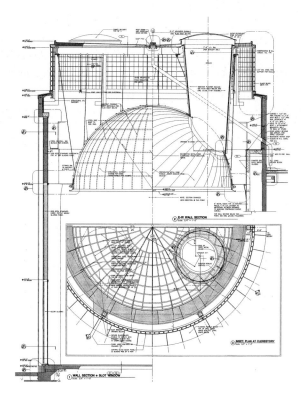

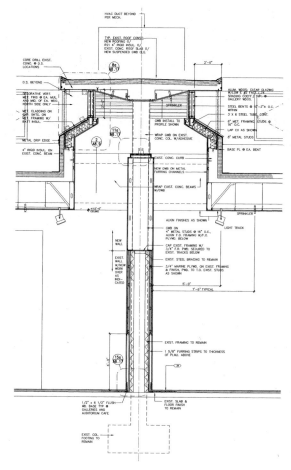

▲ Plan and wall section at entrance rotunda with oculus skylight.

▶ Typical wall section through permanent exhibition galleries.

◀ Section through
auditorium and permanent
exhibition galleries.

▲ Rendered section illustrating
relationship of skylight to
exhibition galleries.

MUSEO DE ARTE DE PUERTO RICO,
Santurce, San Juan, Puerto Rico

THE MUSEUM GROUP: OTTO REYES CASANOVA AIA, LUIS GUTIERREZ AIA (SAN JUAN), AND RKK&G
MUSEUM AND CULTURAL FACILITIES CONSULTANTS, ARCHITECTS (2000)

Background and Purpose

In 1996, the Commonwealth of Puerto Rico, through two of its agencies, the Puerto Rican Tourism Company and the Government Development Bank for Puerto Rico, funded the planning and construction of the Museo de Arte de Puerto Rico (Puerto Rico Museum of Art). The goal was to create a state-of-the-art museum dedicated to the display and study of Puerto Rico's visual arts and provide up-to-date facilities for major international exhibitions, thus increasing interest in the island as a vacationers' destination.

Site Planning

The site chosen, at the time used mostly as an outdoor parking lot, was the former 1922 Municipal Hospital building in Santurce, near the headquarters of the Government Development Bank for Puerto Rico and the Luis A. Ferré Center for the Performing Arts (Bellas Artes).

The colonial-like two-story building is made of concrete, with a classical cement/stucco façade. It has a partial basement and had been organized into a series of nursing wards flanking a main center structure. Its plan was suited for adaptation into gallery space and museum receiving facilities.

The building was restored, and a new addition doubled the size of the existing footprint. The rest of the site was developed as a passive landscape, offering outdoor potential for other programs. On-site parking accommodates the needs of the museum staff as well as those of employees from nearby government office buildings.

View of garden entrance to museum.
Photo: J. Betancourt

SIGNIFICANT ISSUES

Program
An art museum with the expected benefit of promoting tourism

Unique design concerns
Special needs of an art museum located in a tropical climate

Site planning
Combining new and restored construction with extensive landscape development

Mechanical systems
Humidity control in a tropical climate

Interiors
Emphasis on materials and finishes, using locally quarried marbles and granites unique to the site

Wayfinding
A central Great Hall to provide a visual, self-orienting guide to the visitor

Renovation/adaptive reuse
Conversion of an abandoned structure into a state-of-the-art museum

Financing
A private, not-for-profit institution supported, in part, by government economic development agencies

The site plan notes the following features:

- A major entrance and decorative fountain, surrounded by an access drive from the existing street

- An additional approach leading to a porte cochere entrance to the museum's Great Hall for ceremonial occasions.

- A service drive entrance and loading dock, this approach also providing access to the site's new above-ground parking

- Extensive landscape improvements for concerts, festivals, public events, and outdoor recreation

View of Great Hall/atrium, looking toward garden entrance.

Design
The museum contains the following spaces:

- The former hospital structure, now the main entrance to the museum and housing the permanent collection in 14 exhibition galleries.

- The East Wing—the new construction —a five-story building with a three-story atrium as its Great Hall.

- The Great Hall/atrium, next to:
A 450-seat multipurpose theater
The book/gift shop
Food service facilities

- Two 5,000-sq-ft exhibition galleries overlooking the Great Hall. These are equipped for maximum flexibility and prepared by size and design to accept special or international visiting exhibitions.

- The Family Gallery, located below the Great Hall, with direct access from the museum's landscaped gardens. Hands-on educational exhibitions feature works of art from the permanent collection.

- The education department, consisting of the following:
Four art studios
Two classrooms
Seminar room
Student gallery
Student lunch room
Faculty/volunteer lounge
Multimedia computer laboratory

- A conservation laboratory, art and general storage facilities, and administrative offices.

- A five-acre garden. When complete, it will include nearly 106,000 native trees, shrubs, ground covers, and flowers.

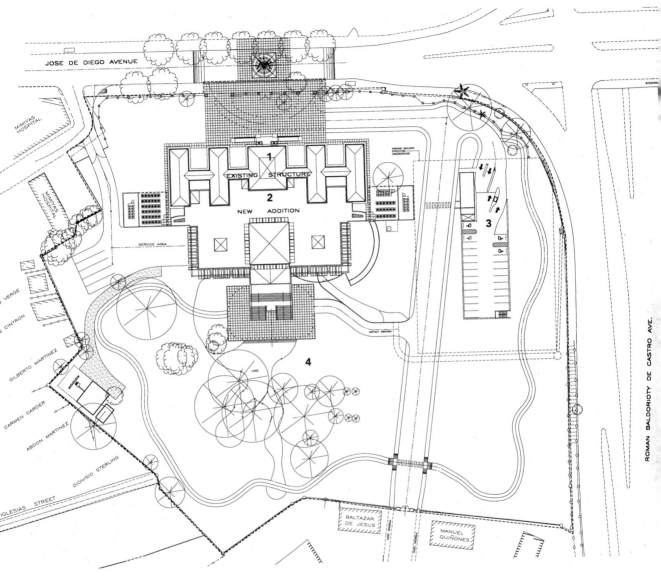

Site plan.
1 *Existing restored*
   Municipal Hospital
2 *New construction*
3 *Parking facility*
4 *Public park*

Aerial view of abandoned former Municipal Hospital.

Receiving and Storage

The receiving and loading-dock area is the single entry and exit for the museum, with 24-hour maintenance and security. All materials and supplies, including works of art, enter and all discarded food service trash leaves the building from this area.

Major activities located here include the following:

- Loading dock for at least two trucks, trailers, or other vehicles, with other loading-dock leveling platforms.

- Separate, isolated refrigerated interim trash room, primarily for food-service trash.

- Security officer and central security and life safety monitoring facility.

- Entry point and time-card board for maintenance and security personnel. Administrative and professional staff may also use this entry.

- Registrar's office, condition report and photo record spaces.

- Locker rooms, with toilet and shower facilities.

- Storage rooms for:
  General supplies
  Book/gift shop merchandise
  Food-service supplies

- Art storage with strict conformance to

the highest standards of temperature and humidity control. Separate storage rooms for:
Three-dimensional art
Paintings
Paper (photos, prints, drawings, etc.)
Organic materials

Registrar

The location and quality of the registrar's office is a major factor in a museum's ability to attract important individual art loans and exhibitions from private and institutional sources.

The Registrar's office includes the following:

- Private office with adjoining secretarial space.

- Workshop with:
  Rolling racks for the interim storage of stretched canvases and frames.
  Work counters with above and below shelving and storage for supplies.
  Two wash basins/sinks.
  Airtight and dustproof storage cabinets for small objects and paper art.
  Wood-cushioned vertical storage racks for flat material.
  Photo room for immediate record photography of incoming and outgoing art. This facility is designed for the required condition report function and is not meant to be a fully realized photo studio.
  Fumigation room to be used when required by the registrar's office or the art conservation staff.
  Crate storage (a large space needed to safely store oversized shipping materials). The arrival of a traveling exhibition will generate the need for this facility.

Security

For a museum to attract important artworks, and exhibitions from overseas, its security department must meet precisely the standards set by the lending institutions and insurance underwriters covering the loan programs. The most sophisticated and efficient surveillance is required, and security and surveillance systems must be maintained and serviced to a high standard.

The main security booth/station typically has all security and life safety systems reporting by:

- Video surveillance

- Motion detection

- Smoke detection

- Light detection

- Sprinkler systems

- Microwave monitoring, if required

This is the central monitoring site for all satellite systems.

Book/Gift Shop

Traditionally, museums have assumed that book/gift shops were no more than conveniences for the visitor. In the last two decades, it has become increasingly clear that museum shops are important mechanisms for significantly increasing an institution's financial stability and extending to the public a vast array of educational tools that increase understanding and appreciation of art.

The museum shop is organized in the following manner:

- Cash counter and control. At the entrance, with full visual surveillance of the entire shop, is the cash counter and an island featuring high-end merchandise that includes jewelry, scarves, neckties, and special products of a unique nature.

- Books and periodicals—art publications originating in the museum and outside.

- Music and videos.

- Postcards, calendars, notepaper, other paper products.

- Toys, educational games and products. Recognizing that large numbers of schoolchildren will be visiting, it is necessary to provide inexpensive and easily purchased items such as pens, pencils, crayons, and coloring books.

- Posters and prints. Museum generated, including special printings of the poster art of Puerto Rico.

- Clothing. T-shirts, belts, socks.

- Software and computer products.

- Frames and mats.

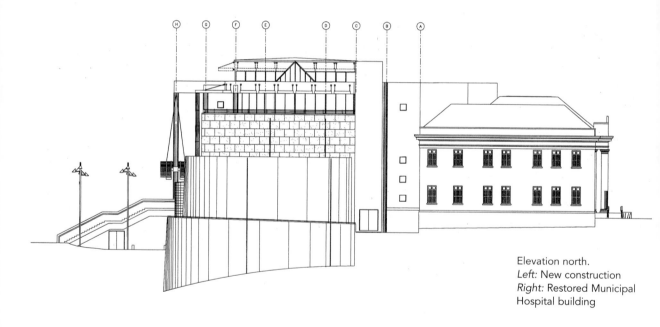

Elevation north.
Left: New construction
Right: Restored Municipal Hospital building

Elevation west.
Restored Municipal Hospital façade

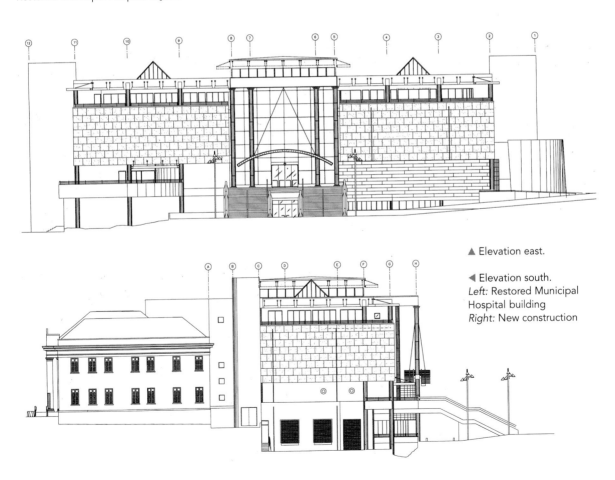

▲ Elevation east.

◀ Elevation south.
Left: Restored Municipal
Hospital building
Right: New construction

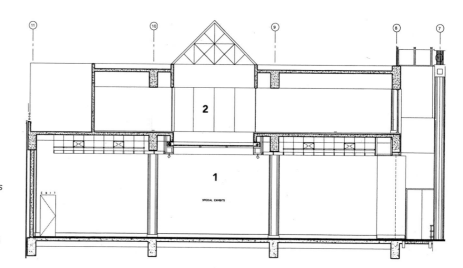

Section through special
exhibition gallery.
1 *Special exhibition gallery*
2 *Raised skylight providing
controlled natural light.
Horizontal opaque shades
can eliminate all natural
light.*

▼ View of special exhibition
gallery.

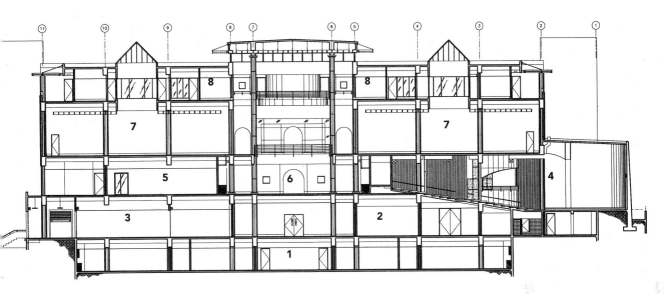

Section AA.
1 *Education Center*
2 *Conservation*
3 *Receiving, registrar, and security*
4 *Auditorium*
5 *Café, restaurant, and book shop*
6 *Great Hall/atrium*
7 *Special exhibition gallery*
8 *Administration.*

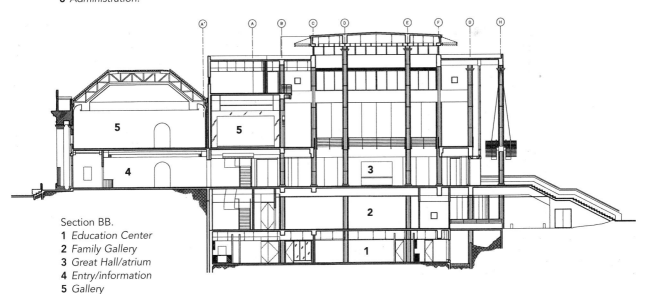

Section BB.
1 *Education Center*
2 *Family Gallery*
3 *Great Hall/atrium*
4 *Entry/information*
5 *Gallery*

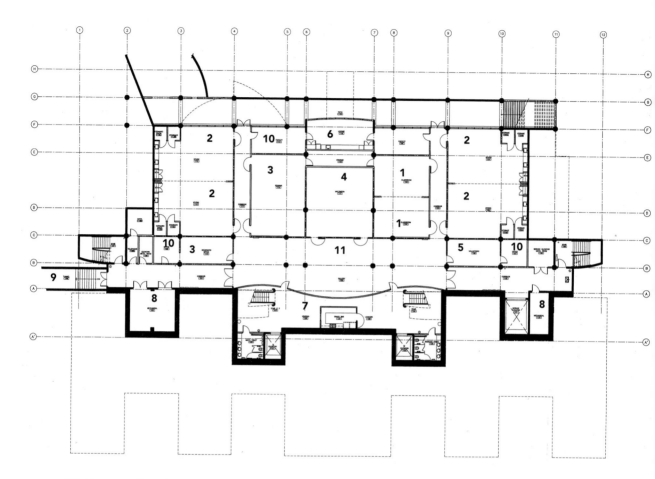

Level 1: Classroom floor plan.
 1 *Classroom*
 2 *Studio art*
 3 *Seminar room*
 4 *Multimedia studio*
 5 *Volunteers*
 6 *Staff lounge*
 7 *Snack bar*
 8 *Mechanical*
 9 *Entry from parking garage*
10 *Offices*
11 *Gallery*

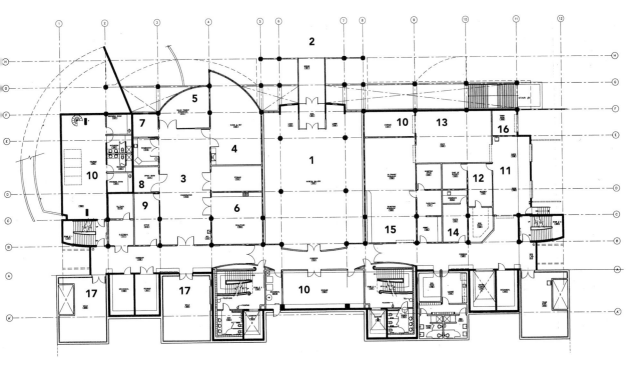

▲ Level 2: Registrar and conservation.

1 Family Gallery
2 Entry to Family Gallery from park
3 Conservation Center
4 Conservation clean and wet area
5 Paintings conservation
6 Sculpture conservation
7 Conservation laboratory
8 Spray room
9 Office
10 Storage
11 Loading dock/receiving
12 Security officer
13 Crate storage
14 Photo studio for condition reports
15 Registrar
16 Trash room
17 Vault

Conservation studio.
1 *Conservation studio with heat suction and worktables*
2 *Painting conservation studio*
3 *Conservation studio with worktables and fiberglass paper bath*
4 *Storage*
5 *Conservation studio for sculpture and three-dimensional objects*
6 *Office*
7 *Spray booth*
8 *Photo studio*
9 *Laboratory*

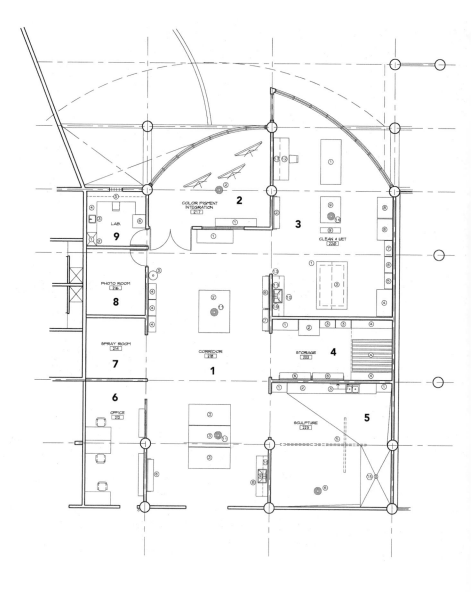

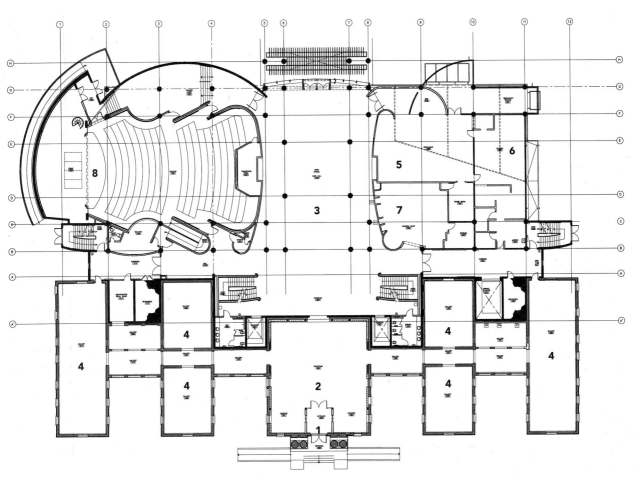

Level 3: Main floor.
1 Entry
2 Information/orientation
3 Great Hall/atrium
4 Gallery
5 Café/restaurant
6 Kitchen
7 Book/gift shop
8 Auditorium

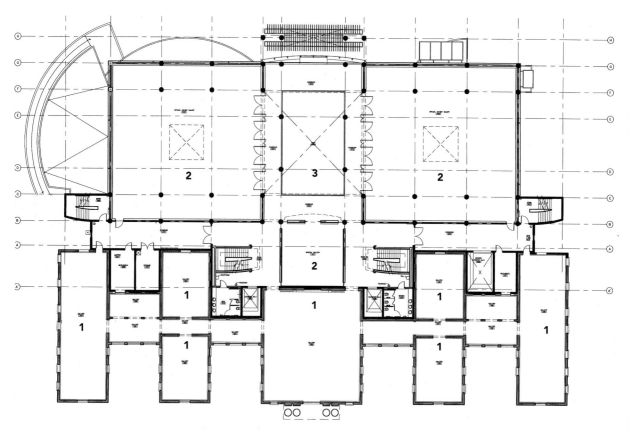

▲ Level 4: Main galleries.
1 *Gallery*
2 *Special exhibition gallery*
3 *Open atrium*

▶ Views of typical gallery in restored Municipal Hospital building.
Photos: J. Betancourt

▼ Typical gallery soffit lighting details. Note indirect fluorescent light source within soffit. Where necessary, ductwork can be enclosed in soffit, as shown in detail on right. Light track is recessed in bottom of soffit.

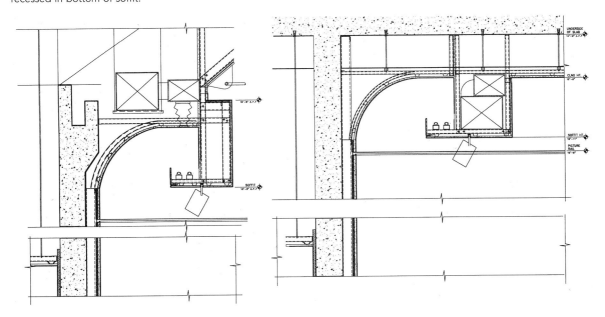

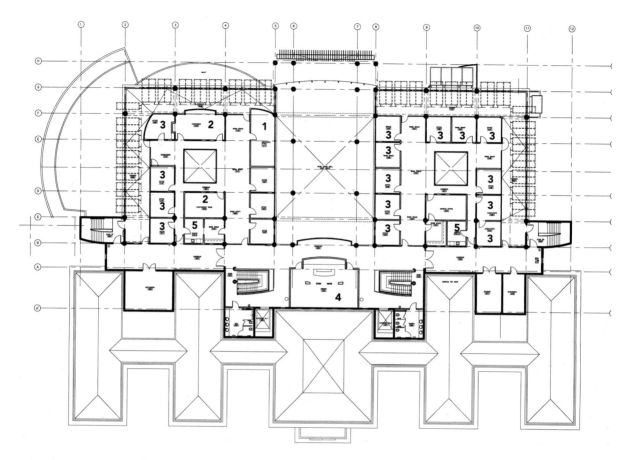

Level 5: Administration floor.
1 *Director's office*
2 *Conference room*
3 *Office*
4 *Library*
5 *Pantry*

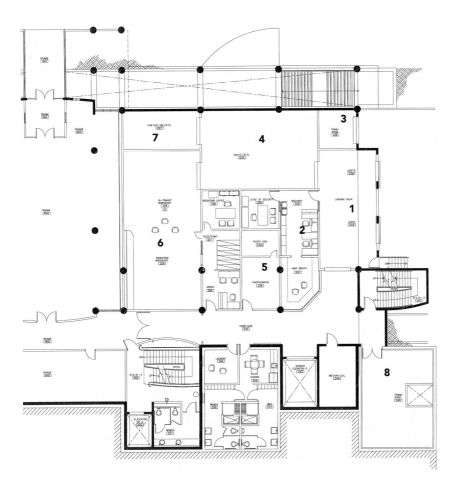

Receiving, security, and registrar.
1 Loading dock
2 Security
3 Trash room
4 Crate storage
5 Photograph studio for condition reports
6 Registrar
7 Fumigation room (necessary in tropical climates)
8 Frame shop

NAOSHIMA CONTEMPORARY ART MUSEUM,
Naoshima, Japan
TADAO ANDO & ASSOCIATES, ARCHITECTS (1992, 1994)

Site

The Naoshima Contemporary Art Museum is both museum and hotel. It is located within a national park on the island of Naoshima, in the Inland Sea of Japan. More than half the museum's volume is underground so as not to intrude on the scenic surroundings.

The museum's galleries, stepped terraces, and plazas all face the Inland Sea. Above the museum, hotel guest rooms occupy two stories.

Design and Circulation

Upon arrival by boat, visitors are met with a stepped plaza that functions as both museum and hotel entrance. In addition, the plaza serves as a stage for outdoor performances. Only after visitors climb the plaza steps do the rubble-stone walls of the museum come into view.

SIGNIFICANT ISSUES

Program
Combined small art museum and hotel

Unique design concerns
Using the environment as part of the architecture

Site planning/access
A unique setting and unusual means of access

View of north side of main building with peaked glass roof over main gallery.
Photo: Mitsuo Matsuoka

Entering the building, visitors find themselves in a linear underground gallery more than two stories high, 150 ft long, and 25 ft wide. Rising through the entire structure is a cylindrical gallery. An oculus, capping the cylinder, is contained within a high glass core, providing natural daylight deep in the interior of the gallery.

An annex, providing additional hotel rooms, museum offices, and a visitor's café, was completed in 1994. At its entrance is a cascade waterfall and a large garden enclosed by a stone wall.

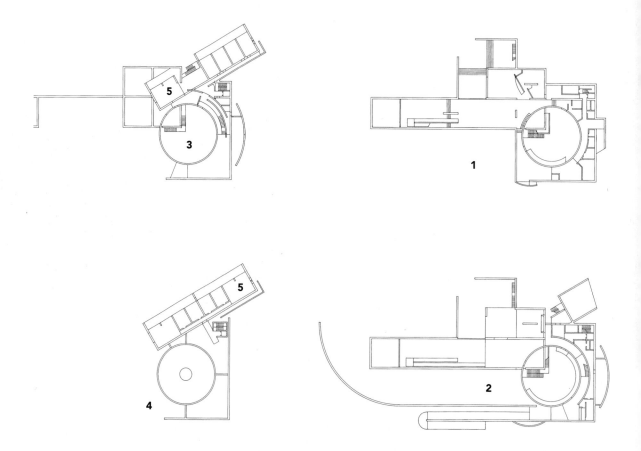

Floor plans. The great cylindrical gallery begins at the basement floor and rises through the building to the roof; the rectangular galleries are stacked one above the other. The two floors of the small hotel rest atop the museum.

1 *Basement floor*
2 *First floor*
3 *Second floor*
4 *Third floor*
5 *Hotel floors*

Grand Louvre.
Aerial view at night.
Photo: Alfred Wolf

Gallery

▶ Entrance to the Linsky
Galleries at the Metropolitan
Museum of Art.
Photo: Stan Ries

▼ Metropolitan Museum
of Art.
The American Wing and
Garden Court.

Aerial view of Metropolitan
Museum of Art in Central Park.

Gallery

J. Paul Getty Museum.
Entrance overlooking entry plaza.
Photo: Scott Frances/Esto

Miho Museum.
View from approach tunnel of Reception Pavilion.
Photo: Kiyohiko Higashide

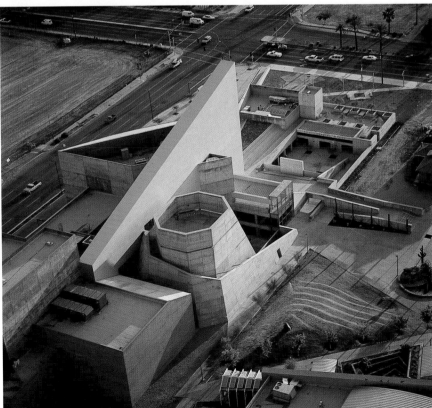

▲ Kiasma Museum for
Contemporary Art.
Overall view with service
entrance on left and
cafeteria at first floor on
right.
Photo: Paul Warchol

◄ Arizona Science Center.
Aerial view.
Photo: Timothy Hursley

Sainsbury Wing, National Gallery.
Early Renaissance and Northern European
galleries. Note sequence and size of door
openings, emphasizing the perspective vista.
Photo: Phil Starling

◀ Frye Art Museum.
Entrance rotunda. Note
clerestory light and oculus
skylight.

▼ Frye Art Museum.
Night view of entrance
rotunda.
Photo: Eckert & Eckert

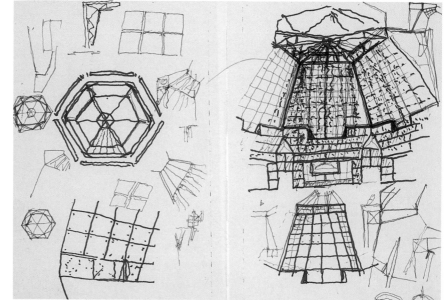

▶ U.S. Holocaust Memorial Museum.
Conceptual drawings by James Ingo Freed.

▼ San Francisco Museum of Modern Art.
View of museum from Howard Street.
Photo: Robert Canfield

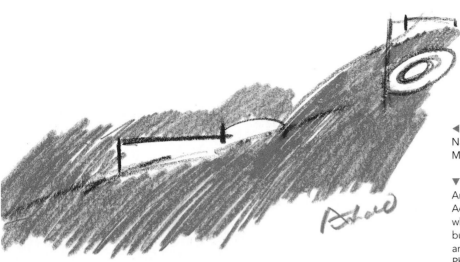

◀ Conceptual sketch of Naoshima Contemporary Art Museum by Tadao Ando.

▼ Naoshima Contemporary Art Museum.
Aerial view with entrance wharf on left, the main building in the center, and the annex addition on the right.
Photo: Mitsuo Matsuoka

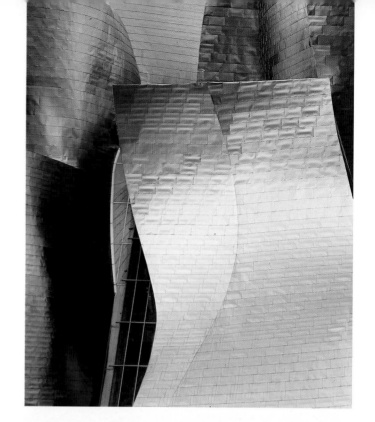

▶ Approach to the
Guggenheim/Bilbao from
the city.
Photo: Timothy Hursley

▼ Aerial view of
Guggenheim/Bilbao.
Photo: Timothy Hursley

Rock and Roll Hall of Fame
and Museum.
Night view.
Photo: Timothy Hursley

▶ Museo de Arte de Ponce. Night view of José Compeche Wing.

▼ American Air Museum. View of museum from airfield at Duxton, England.

◀ McCord Museum of Canadian History. Entrance façade on Rue Victoria. Original 1906 wing on left; new 1992 wing on right.

▼ Route 66 Museum. View of entry structure incorporating glass block, neon signs, and other materials typical of Route 66. Photo: Hedrich-Blessing

Gallery

▶ Beyeler Foundation
Museum.
Exterior elevation.
Photo: M. Denance

▼ View of main façade
of Minnesota Children's
Museum. Glazed towers
at ends mark exhibition
galleries.
Photo: Peter Kerze

◀ Museo de Arte de Puerto Rico.
Former Municipal Hospital restored as entrance to museum.

▼ Rose Center for Earth and Space.
Night view from West 81st Street.
Photo: American Museum of Natural History

Gallery

▶ Children's Museum of Houston. Entrance to museum.

▼ Central Park Zoo. View of temperate territory zone.

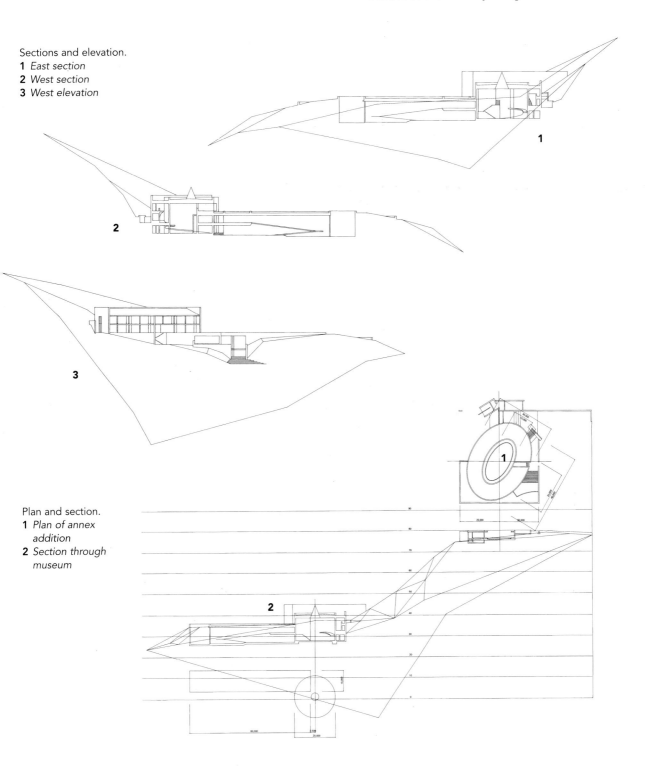

Sections and elevation.
1 *East section*
2 *West section*
3 *West elevation*

Plan and section.
1 *Plan of annex addition*
2 *Section through museum*

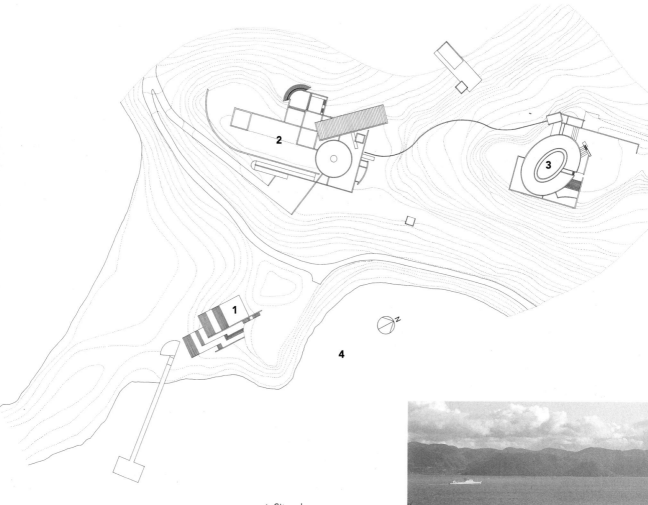

▲ Site plan.
1 *Wharf and entrance terrace*
2 *Main building of museum*
3 *Annex addition and guest rooms*
4 *Japan's Inland Sea*

▶ Landscaped roof over main building.
Photo: Hiroshi Ueda

◀ The oval-shaped annex surrounds a central water feature with rooftop plantings.
Photo: Tomio Ohashi

▲ Central gallery in main building.
Photo:Hiroshi Ueda

◀ Central gallery, virtually underground, with natural light provided by peaked glass cone skylight.
Photo: Mitsuo Matsuok

DIE AND LIVE
SHIT AND LIVE
PISS AND LIVE
EAT AND LIVE
SLEEP AND LIVE
LOVE AND LIVE

SPEAK AND LIVE
LIE AND LIVE
HEAR AND LIVE

SING AND LIVE
SCREAM AND LIVE
YOUNG AND LIVE
OLD AND LIVE
CUT AND LIVE
RUN AND LIVE
STAY AND LIVE
PLAY AND LIVE

SUCK AND LIVE
COME AND LIVE

GUGGENHEIM MUSEUM, *Bilbao, Spain*
FRANK O. GEHRY, ARCHITECT (1997)

Background and Program

In the last two decades, with the decline of the shipbuilding, steel, and iron refining industries, Bilbao elected to emphasize culture in its efforts to attract new businesses and create a tourist industry. The museum is a major element of a comprehensive urban redevelopment program and architectural renaissance. Because of its location in an industrial corridor, it provides the focus for numerous other large-scale improvements that are transforming the city.

SIGNIFICANT ISSUES

Program
The museum as centerpiece for an urban redevelopment project

Site planning
A riverfront site, once dedicated to industry and shipbuilding, to become a cultural center

Structural system
Innovative large-span columns to free exhibition spaces

Materials
Unique use of titanium zinc roofing

International challenges
Worldwide outreach of famed New York museum

Financing
The entire capital and operating costs of the museum to be undertaken by government

Aerial view of Guggenheim/Bilbao.
Photo: David Herald/Guggenheim

Plans for a new cultural institution for Bilbao date back to the late 1980s, when the Basque administration began formulating a redevelopment program for the city. A museum of modern and contemporary art was conceived to be an essential part of this plan.

In 1991, Basque officials approached the Solomon R. Guggenheim Foundation to propose that it participate in Bilbao's redevelopment program. A preliminary agreement was reached that year, leading to the establishment of the Guggenheim Museum Bilbao Foundation to manage the new institution. The Basque administration brings to the relationship its political and cultural authority, land, and financial resources for both capital improvements and total operating support. The Solomon R. Guggenheim Foundation provides the core collection for the new museum and offers curatorial and management expertise as well as programming.

Site

The 301,000-sq-ft Guggenheim Museum Bilbao creates a dramatic and highly visible landmark for Bilbao. It stands on an irregularly shaped site that marks the center of a cultural triangle formed by the Museo de Belles Artes, the Universidad de Deusto, and the Old Town Hall.

A water garden surrounds the building, linking the site with the river and promenade. The auditorium, restaurant, and book/gift shop are accessible from the main plaza as well as from within the museum, enabling them to operate independently of the museum's hours and to support the urban life of Bilbao.

Design and Materials

The museum is composed of interconnected building blocks, clad in limestone, which house exhibition spaces and public facilities. These are (in sq ft):

- Galleries   113,520
- Public spaces   26,900
- Library   2,150
- Auditorium (350 seats)   6,500
- Curatorial and administrative office   12,900
- Retail and bookshop   4,000
- Restaurant   5,000
- Café   2,600

Individual building components are unified into a single architectural composition by the Guggenheim Museum Bilbao's signature roof, a composition of twisting, curving, and jutting forms made of titanium—a metal rarely used in construction, but suited to the saltwater marine environment of Bilbao.

The central feature of Gehry's design is a 165-ft-high atrium, more than one and a half times the height of the rotunda of Frank Lloyd Wright's building in New York. Flooded with light from glazed openings in the roof, the atrium is served by two glass enclosed elevators and curvilinear pedestrian catwalks that connect with two stairways, providing views of the river and the city and hills beyond.

Galleries

Three levels of galleries are organized around the central atrium. Included are those designed for the presentation of large-scale works of art and site-specific installations that could not be mounted in more conventional museums.

Lighting

Natural light enters galleries through skylights with adjustable blinds whose spectrum-controlled glass limits the penetration of ultraviolet light. Galleries are artificially illuminated by a lighting system mounted on exposed catwalks suspended from the ceiling.

Site plan.

Conceptual sketches of
Guggenheim/Bilbao by
Frank Gehry.

▼ Entrance to
Guggenheim/Bilbao.
Photo: David Herald/
Guggenheim

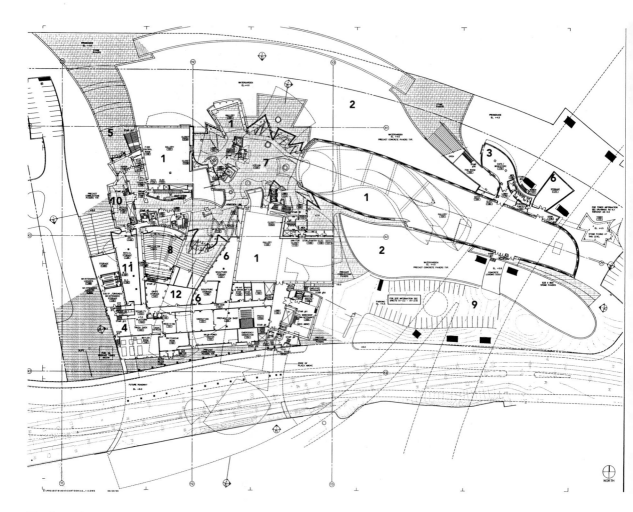

First floor plan
 1 Gallery
 2 Water garden
 3 Café/bookstore
 4 Loading dock/receiving
 5 Entry
 6 Storage
 7 Atrium
 8 Auditorium
 9 Parking
10 Retail
11 Retail storage
12 Crate storage

View of long gallery on first floor, with Richard Serra sculpture.
Photo: Timothy Hursley

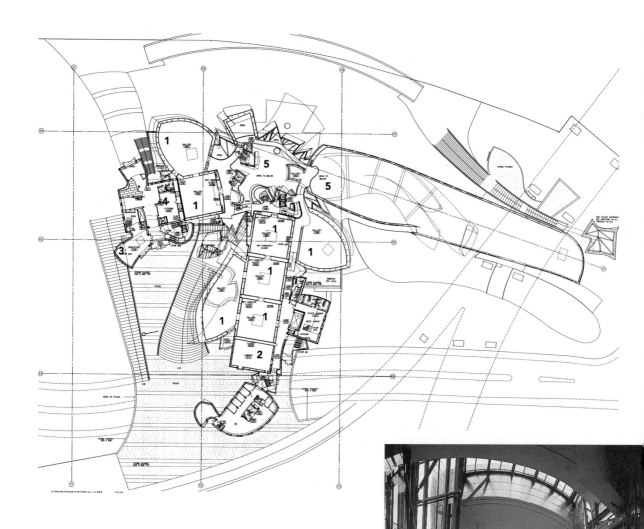

▲ Second floor plan.
1 *Gallery*
2 *Library*
3 *Bookstore*
4 *Kitchen*
5 *Open to below*

▶ View of entrance atrium during construction.
Photo: Timothy Hursley

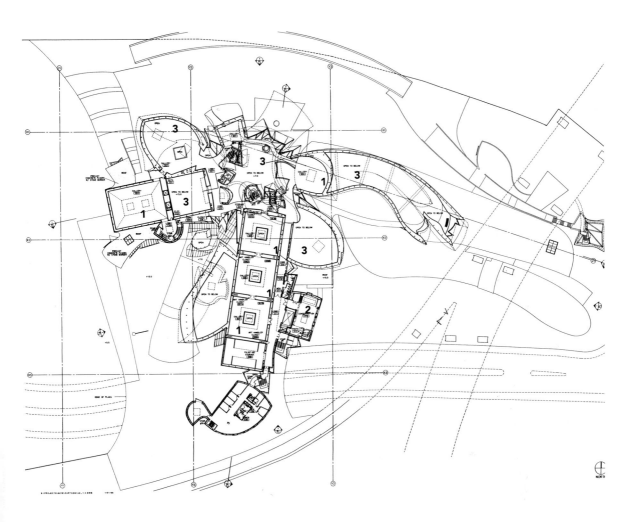

Third floor plan.
1 *Gallery*
2 *Conservation*
3 *Open to below*

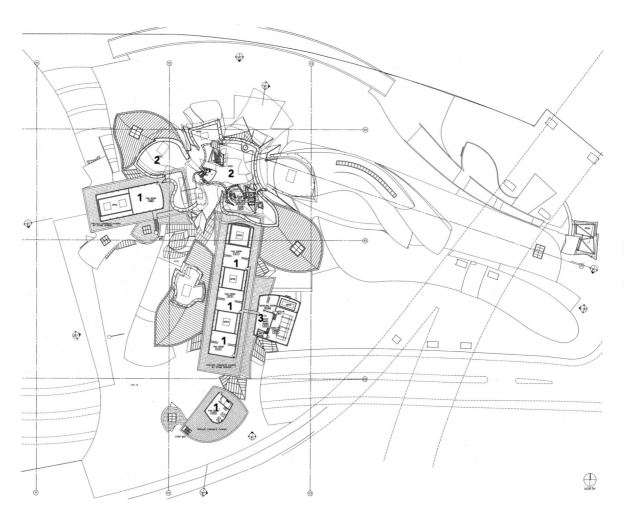

Fourth floor plan.
1 *Fan room*
2 *Open to below*
3 *Mechanical room*

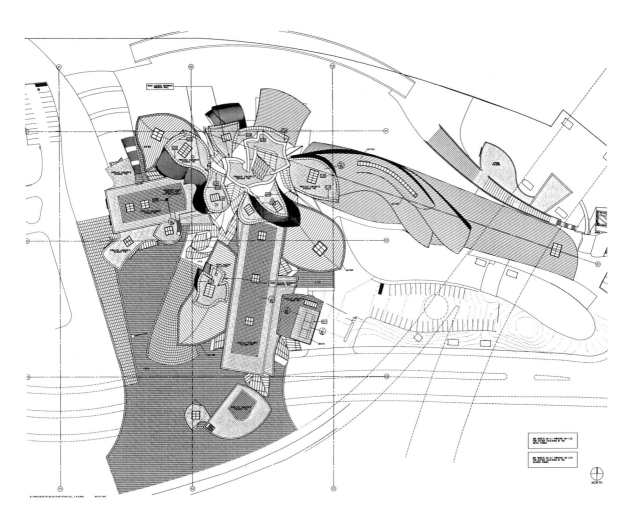

Roof plan.

ART MUSEUMS

Section AA.
1 *Atrium*
2 *Gallery*
3 *Kitchen*
4 *Storage*

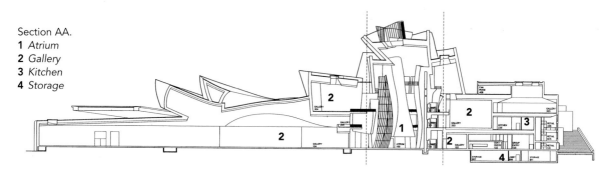

Section BB.
1 *Atrium*
2 *Gallery*
3 *Library*
4 *Administration*

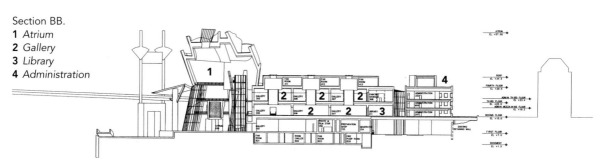

Section CC.
1 *Group entry*
2 *Auditorium*
3 *Gallery*
4 *Restaurant*

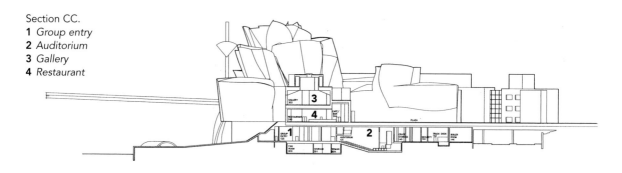

Section DD.
1 *Auditorium*
2 *Plaza*
3 *Gallery*
4 *Storage*
5 *Maintenance*

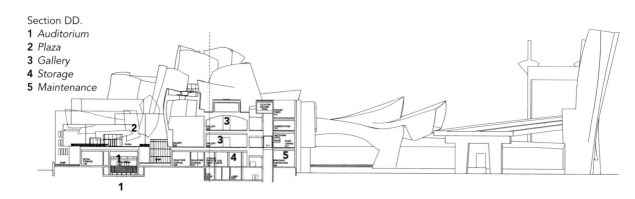

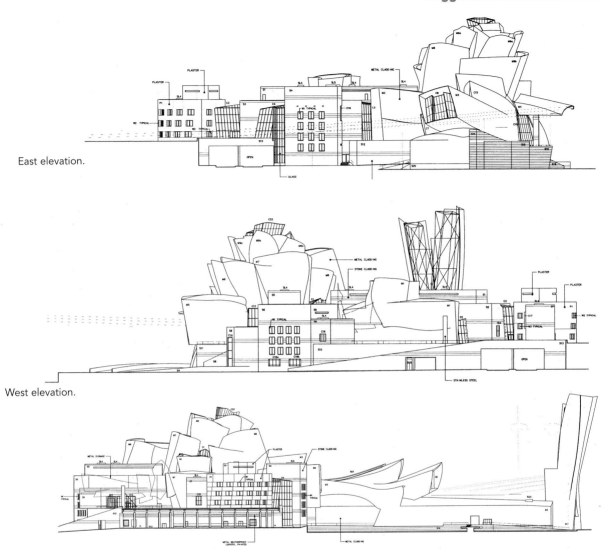

East elevation.

West elevation.

South elevation.

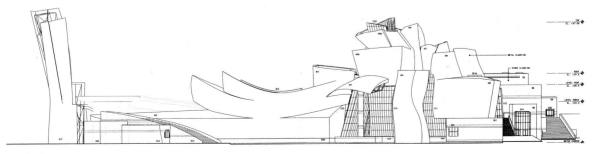

North elevation.

SAN FRANCISCO MUSEUM OF MODERN ART
(SFMOMA), *San Francisco, California*
MARIO BOTTA, ARCHITECT, IN ASSOCIATION WITH HELMUTH, OBATA AND KASSABAUM (COMPLETED 1995)

Background and Purpose

The 225,000-sq-ft building is the second-largest single structure in the United States devoted to modern art (after New York's Museum of Modern Art). It replaces the museum's former location at the War Memorial Veterans Building in San Francisco's Civic Center, its home since its founding in 1935.

Site

SFMOMA is located in a former skid-row neighborhood known as SOMA (South of Market Street). Designated an urban redevelopment site by the city, the area now features other buildings for art by well-known architects.

In the Yerba Buena Gardens, opposite the new museum on Third Street and near the Moscone Convention Center, are

- The Center for the Arts' Visual Art Center, designed by Fumihiko Maki

- The Center for the Arts Theater, a

comprehensive performing-arts complex designed by James Stewart Polshek

Design

The building features a stepped-back brick and stone façade distinguished by a soaring truncated cylinder emerging from the roof. To the rear, a five-story tower houses galleries as well as the museum's curatorial and administrative offices. The sides of the rear of the building have been designed to anticipate needs for future additional gallery space and program development.

Other key features of the building include the following.

- 50,000 sq ft dedicated to galleries, doubling the original space for this purpose. Included are:
Three galleries (about 7,500 sq ft each)
More than 20 separate gallery spaces (each 500 to 3,500 sq ft)

- On the lower or basement level are:
Photography and graphic arts study areas
A 100-seat classroom
A library for more than 65,000 books, catalogs, and periodicals
Storage, receiving, and handling spaces
Mechanical rooms to house the climate-control system

- Opening off the central atrium on the ground floor are:
A 280-seat theater for lectures, symposia, seminars, film and video programs
Two large workshop/studios
A book/gift shop
A café

SIGNIFICANT ISSUES

Program
The creation of the second-largest museum in the United States devoted to twentieth-century art

Site planning
Integration with a major urban redevelopment area

Lighting design
Sophisticated systems to eliminate destructive ultraviolet portions of the spectrum

---

Third Street elevation.
Photo: Robert Cainfield

- The first-floor gallery (16-ft ceilings):
  Houses selections from the permanent collection
  Provides spaces for the architecture and design program

- A second-floor gallery with artificial light and 12-ft ceilings, exhibiting photographs and works on paper

- The top two gallery floors (18-ft and 23.5-ft ceilings) are for:
  Special and temporary exhibitions
  Large-scale contemporary art from the permanent collection
  Multiple-use event space

- On the fourth floor rear, a state-of-the-art facility for art conservation.

- On floors 2 through 4 in the rear, administrative and curatorial offices

Lighting

Ceiling systems—light condensers—combine artificial and natural light for the two top floors of temporary exhibition galleries. These systems eliminate the destructive ultraviolet portions of the spectrum and control footcandle levels.

Conceptual sketches by Mario Botta.

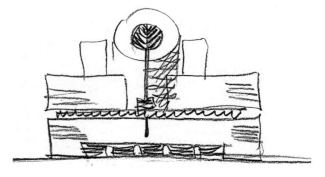

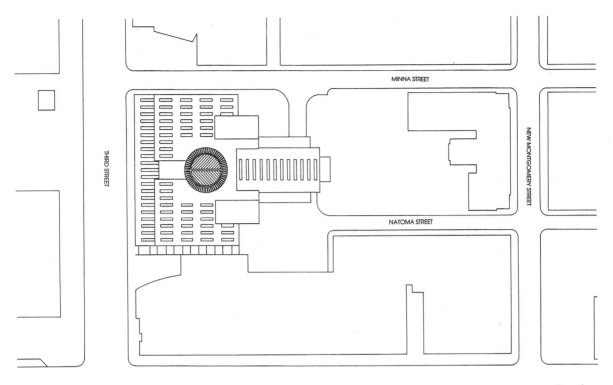

Site plan.

SPACE USAGE

	Area (sq ft)
Exhibition galleries	50,000
Theater	6,200
Education center	3,000
Library	3,800
Conservation laboratory	3,000
Art study and storage	15,000
Book/gift shop	4,000
Multiuse event space	4,200
Central atrium entry	5,000
Café	2,500
Administrative and curatorial offices	22,500

Note: This disposition of space is typical for art museums of this size in urban settings.

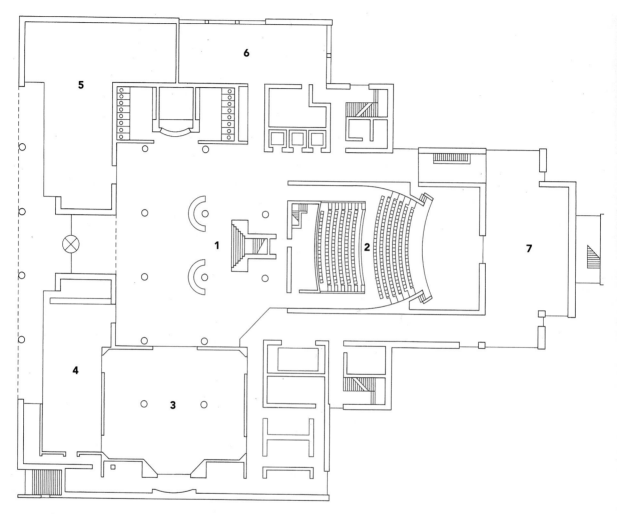

Ground floor.
1 *Atrium/lobby*
2 *Auditorium*
3 *Event space*
4 *Café*
5 *Bookstore*
6 *Classroom*
7 *Loading dock*

Entrance atrium providing
visual orientation to all
exhibition galleries.
Photo: Robert Canfield

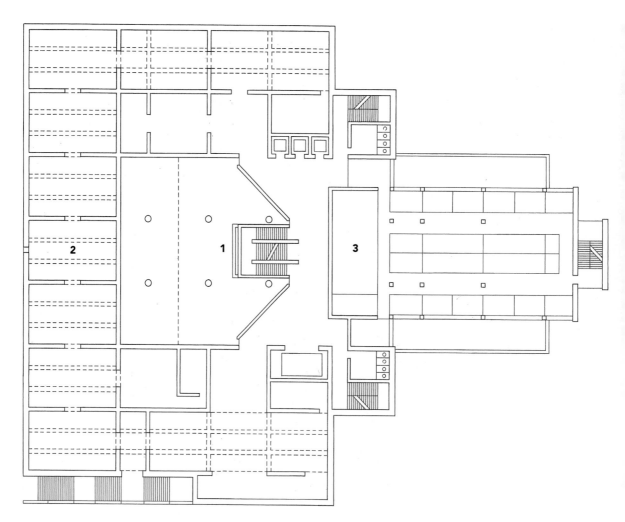

Second floor.
1 *Atrium*
2 *Painting and sculpture,*
architecture, and design
galleries
3 *Offices*

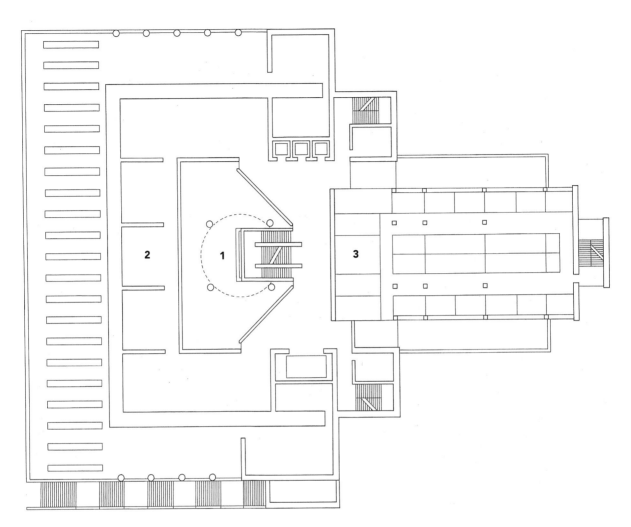

Third floor.
1 Atrium
2 Photography and
  temporary exhibition
  galleries
3 Offices

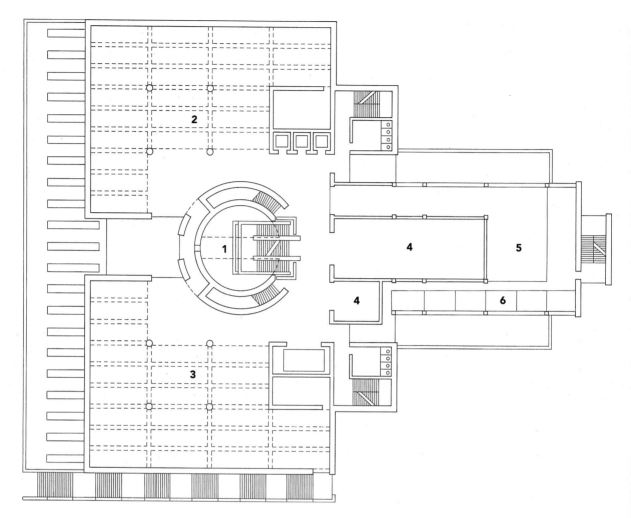

Fourth floor.
1 *Atrium*
2 *Temporary exhibition galleries*
3 *Contemporary art galleries*
4 *Video/media arts*
5 *Conservation lab*
6 *Offices*

View of atrium landing at
fourth floor.
Photo: Robert Canfield

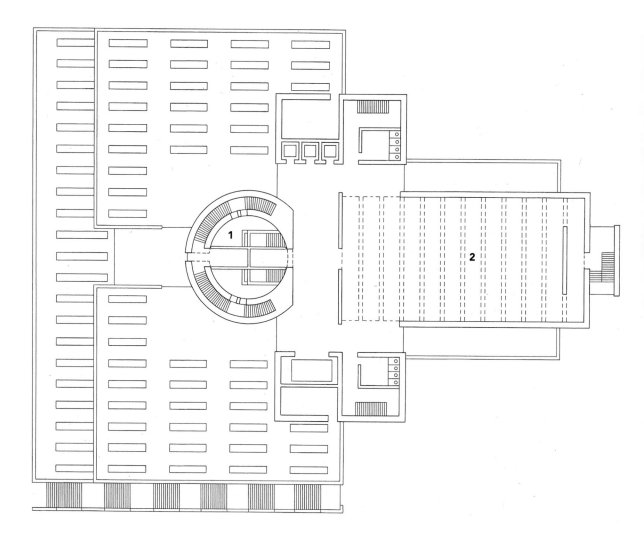

Fifth floor.
1 *Atrium*
2 *Temporary exhibition*
  galleries

View of fifth floor atrium pedestrian bridge connecting exhibition galleries.
Photo: Robert Canfield

View of fifth floor exhibition gallery. Note placement of skylight and track lighting.
Photo: Robert Canfield

ART MUSEUMS

▶ Cross section.

B *Basement, storage*
1 *First floor (café, bookstore, auditorium, classroom, loading dock)*
2 *Second floor (painting and sculpture, architecture and design galleries)*
3 *Third floor (photography and temporary exhibition galleries)*
4 *Fourth floor (temporary, contemporary, and video/media arts galleries)*

▼ Longitudinal section.

B *Basement (storage)*
1 *First floor (offices)*
2 *Second floor (offices)*
3 *Third floor (offices)*
4 *Fourth floor (temporary and contemporary galleries)*
5 *Fifth floor (temporary exhibition galleries)*

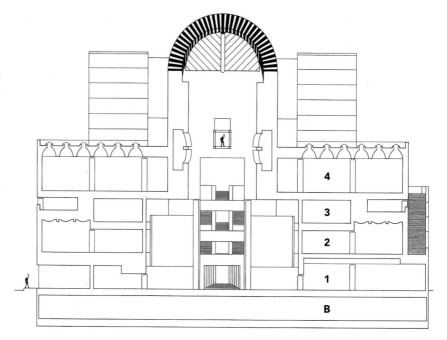

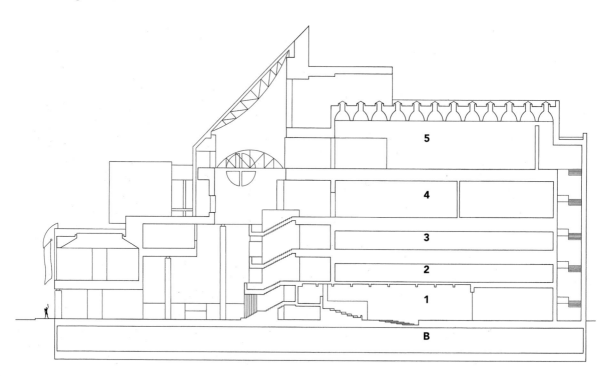

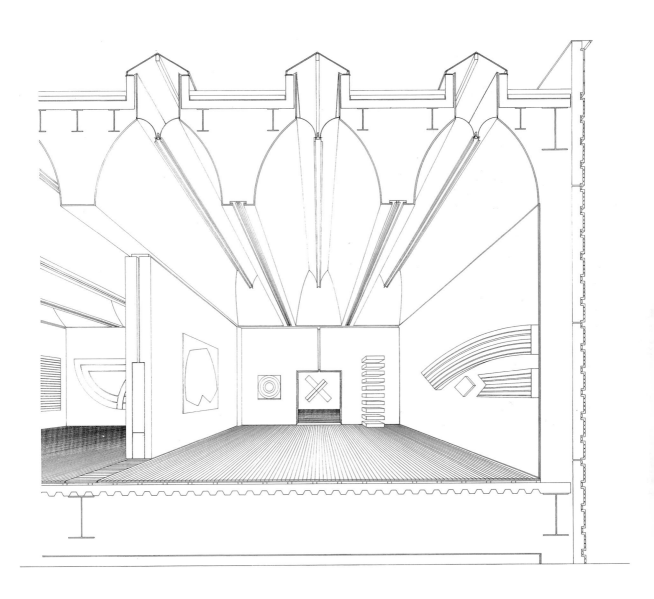

Section through fifth floor exhibition
galleries. Note skylight providing
controlled natural light.

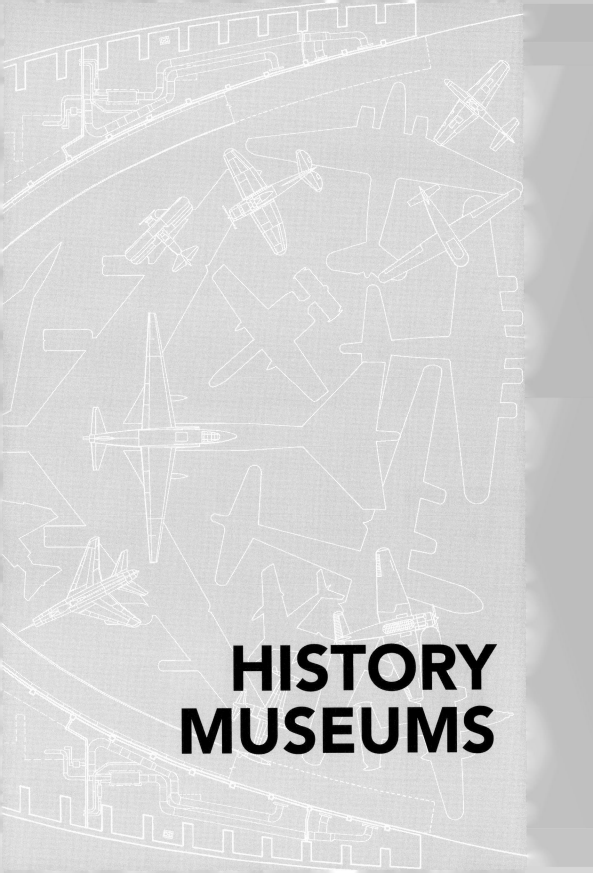

HISTORY
MUSEUMS

THE ROCK AND ROLL HALL OF FAME AND MUSEUM, *Cleveland, Ohio*

I. M. PEI, PEI COBB FREED & PARTNERS, ARCHITECTS (1995)

Site

The Rock and Roll Hall of Fame and Museum was designed to be as spectacular and explosive as rock-and-roll music itself. Situated in downtown Cleveland, overlooking the harbor and Lake Erie beyond, the 143,000-sq-ft building is a focal point of the city's waterfront development. Along with new parklands and a cluster of new museums, it is planned to transform the lakefront into a center for family entertainment and cultural events.

Design

The building is anchored by a 165-ft tower that rises out of Lake Erie. A cantilevered theater projects over the water on one side, balanced on the other by a circular drum conceived as a performance-space-in-the-round.

The tower is connected to a transparent four-sided glass tent that opens onto a paved public plaza. Designed for outdoor entertainment, the plaza creates a welcoming entry to the promenade that threads its way along the Cleveland Harbor.

The plaza is actually the landscaped roof of the museum's main exhibition space, which—tucked below ground to maximize use of the site's change of grade—provides a controlled environment for the museum's highly interactive acoustical and video installations.

Circulation

The interior is organized vertically with floor plates that decrease in size as they ascend, documenting the evolution of rock and roll from its beginnings to the most avant-garde expressions through varied programming and state-of-the-art media presentations.

Visitors rise from the main subgrade exhibition space to the ground-level lobby and then to various programmed spaces on the upper floors. Among these are:

- A bookshop
- A café
- A radio broadcasting studio
- Supplementary exhibition areas
- Two theaters

At the top of a ceremonial stair is the Hall of Fame itself—a contemplative fiber-optic chamber that comprises the

---

SIGNIFICANT ISSUES

Program
To design as spectacular a museum as possible

Circulation
Sequential galleries relate history and folklore

Site planning
A building as focal point of the city's waterfront

Special equipment
Computer-based audio and visual equipment

Acoustic control
A recording and broadcast studio within the museum

The Rock and Roll Hall of Fame and Museum

Exterior view on the edge of North Coast Harbor, overlooking Lake Erie. Photo: Timothy Hursley

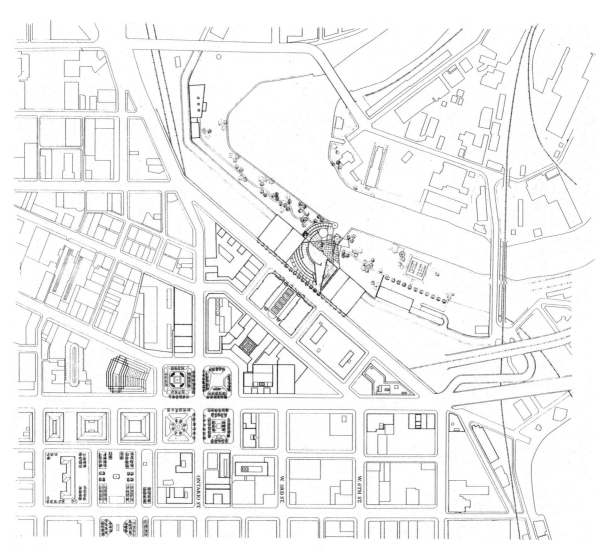

Site plan.

literal and symbolic apex of the entire design.

A rock-and-roll archive, part of the complex, augments the Hall of Fame's standing as a uniquely American icon.

Unique Features

The color and movement of people circulating on the balconies, bridges, stairs, and escalators that crisscross up and down create an exciting visual counterpoint to the rock-and-roll theme. Visitors are not merely spectators but active participants in a design that reveals itself through spaces glimpsed and experienced.

The building is a stage. Animated at night by computer-controlled light, it creates a civic identity as it expresses the museum's energy and openness.

The Rock and Roll Hall of Fame and Museum

◀ Approach to ticketing area within entrance atrium. Photo: Timothy Hursley

▼ Level L (plaza).
1 *Plaza*
2 *Entrance*
3 *Information*
4 *Escalator down to ticketing and main exhibits*
5 *Museum shop*

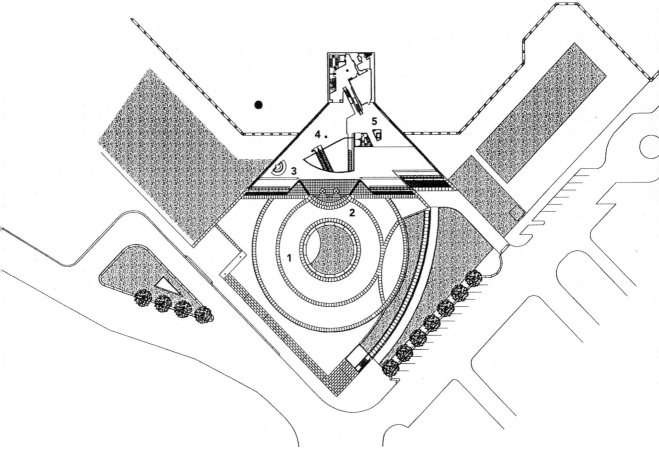

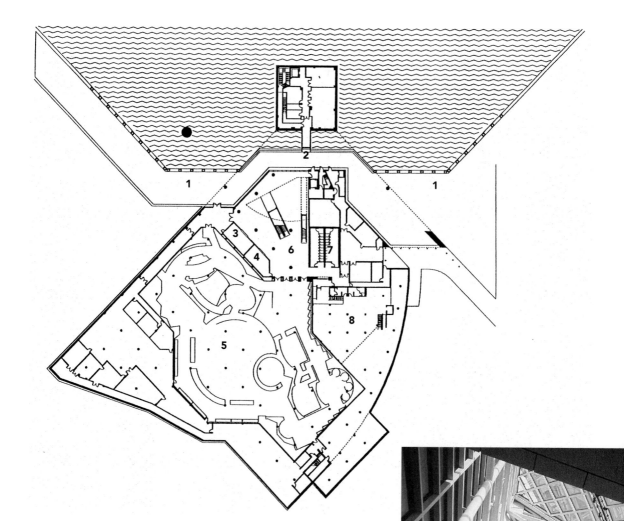

▲ Level G (promenade).
1 Harbor Promenade
2 Harbor Promenade entrance
3 Coat check
4 Ticketing
5 Ahmet M. Ertegun Exhibition
  Hall/Roll Over, Beethoven
6 Escalator up to Level 2 exhibits
7 Rest rooms
8 Offices and archive

▶ Looking skyward within
entrance atrium.
Photo: Timothy Hursley

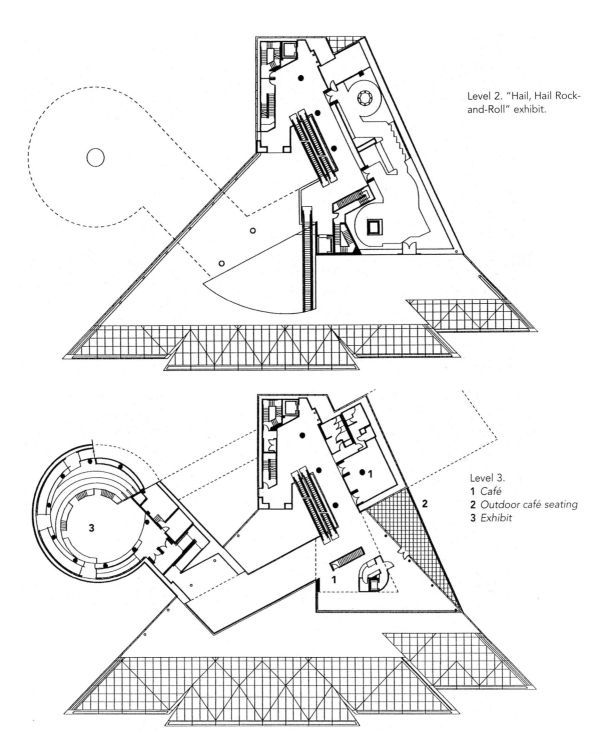

Level 2. "Hail, Hail Rock-and-Roll" exhibit.

Level 3.
1 *Café*
2 *Outdoor café seating*
3 *Exhibit*

Level 5.
1 *Hall of Fame lobby*
2 *DJ booth*
3 *Induction ceremonies
   exhibit*

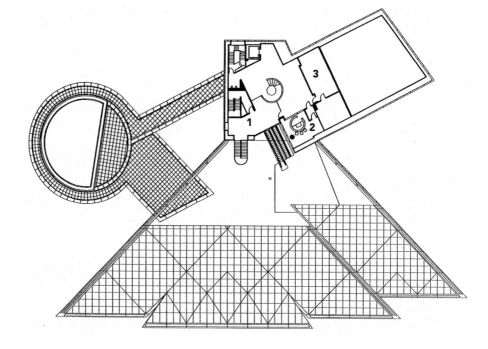

Level 6. Hall of Fame.

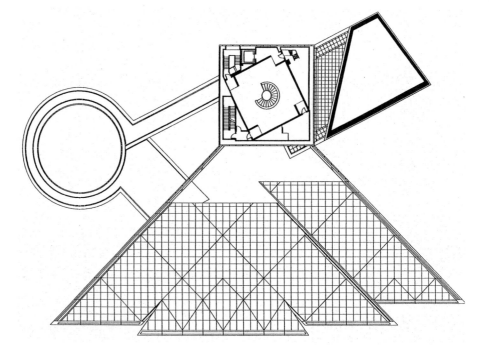

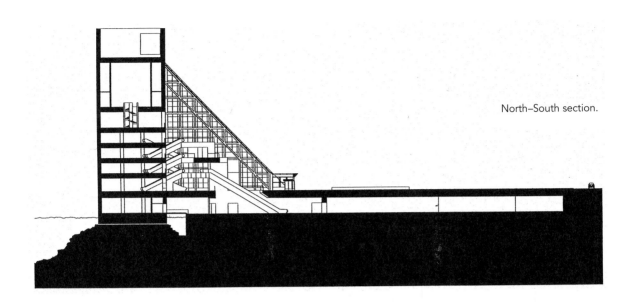

North–South section.

SCHEDULE OF AREAS

	Area (sq ft)		Area (sq ft)
Lower-level promenade		Level 4	
Public circulation	7,800	Public circulation	3,050
Exhibitions	27,600	Auditorium (170 seats)	3,700
Administrative and support	24,300	Exhibitions	1,600
Plaza level		Level 5	
Public circulation	11,000	Public circulation	2,100
Museum book/gift shop	7,800	Exhibitions	700
Level 2		Level 6	
Public circulation	3,350	Public circulation	500
Exhibitions	3,400	Exhibition (Hall of Fame)	1,450
Level 3		Total	143,000
Public circulation	3,350		
Exhibitions	3,200		
Museum café	3,450		
Outdoor terrace café	3,450		

Note: These dimensions are typical of music and performance-related museums of this size.

THE UNITED STATES HOLOCAUST MEMORIAL MUSEUM, *Washington D.C.*

JAMES INGO FREED, FAIA (PEI COBB FREED), ARCHITECT, (1993)

Background and Purpose

The United States Holocaust Memorial Museum was authorized by an act of Congress in 1980 to create a permanent living memorial, funded by private donations and built on federal land, to the more than 10 million people, Christians and Jews alike, who perished in the Holocaust. Located some 400 ft from the Washington Monument, the museum is distinct from the heroic monuments on the National Mall, yet joins them as one of the symbolic presences through which society reaffirms its values.

In response to Washington's urban context, the building is in brick and limestone and of a scale appropriate to its prominent location off the National Mall.

The building houses more than a memorial or a museum. Inside is a living institution dedicated to research, teaching, and the performing arts, as well as to contemplation and commemoration.

Approximately 25 percent of the total space is devoted to permanent exhibits that document the history of the Holocaust, with another 5 percent allotted to temporary or special exhibitions.

Other program spaces include:

- A major research library and archive for scholars

- Curatorial and administrative offices

- A cinema and a theater

- A 10,000-sq-ft conference and education center

- Classrooms

- Ceremonial spaces

- Areas for impromptu group discussions

Design Challenges

Such a programmatically complex building involved significant design challenges:

- How to address a midblock site located between stylistically dissimilar buildings and streets lacking a coherent urban context.

SIGNIFICANT ISSUES

Program
To create a permanent living memorial and museum of the Holocaust of World War II

Unique design concerns
Finding the appropriate symbolic and evocative architecture

Site planning
Site adjacent to the National Mall, in Washington, D.C.

Interior issues
Organization of spaces to present narrative historical exhibits

International challenges
Symbolic significance of architecture to a large international audience

Financing
Public and private partnership for capital and operating costs

The United States Holocaust Memorial Museum

View of U.S. Holocaust
Memorial Museum from
Raoul Wallenberg Place.

- How to create a sober identity for the new museum while joining it to the urban fabric; that is, how to make the museum stand out and yet blend in.

- How to resolve the different agendas of government agencies, museum visitors, and the public at large, while still meeting the requirements of museum administrators, Holocaust survivors, and their descendants, each with individual views of what should be presented and how.

- How to build the museum—how to make stones and cement and mortar speak.

Meaning in Structural Expression

By employing construction techniques from the industrial past, the structure itself plays an important role in evoking memories of that past. For example:

- Structural members are built up from steel plates and double angles riveted together.

- The brick is load bearing; turnbuckles connect tie rods, and the structure is exposed.

The tectonic language is used to explore the fateful misperception that technology is inherently good. The same scientific advances and technological developments embraced in pursuit of a better life were also called upon to perfect the machinery of the Holocaust.

Site

The Museum stands on a prominent site, easily seen by passersby as well as those planning visits. Its main entrance is on 14th Street, a busy artery into and out of the city and a major pedestrian corridor from the Mall to the Bureau of Engraving and Printing.

Fronted by a limestone screen designed to mix with its classic neighbors—the Bureau of Engraving and Printing on one side and the Auditor's Building on the other—the museum is carved to stand out among them, creating an open plaza where school groups and others may gather off the street.

Circulation

From the main entrance, visitors pass through the curved Hall of Flags and are delivered onto a metal stage where sound, texture, and physical reorientation collectively divorce them from the outside world.

They may then take elevators up to the permanent exhibition, or they may proceed into temporary and special exhibition galleries or into the Hall of Witness.

As the Hall of Witness is the beginning of the museum experience, the Hall of Remembrance is its end. Designed for ceremonies and contemplation, it is located on the second floor opposite the permanent exhibition.

From the Hall of Remembrance, visitors descend to the concourse for access to the cinema, performing arts theater, temporary and special exhibition galleries, or the education center.

Because the Holocaust Museum is devoted to an historic event rather than to a display of art, its exhibits are ordered in a linear progression. The journey through time begins with an elevator ride to the fourth floor and descends in rotations around the building as it traces

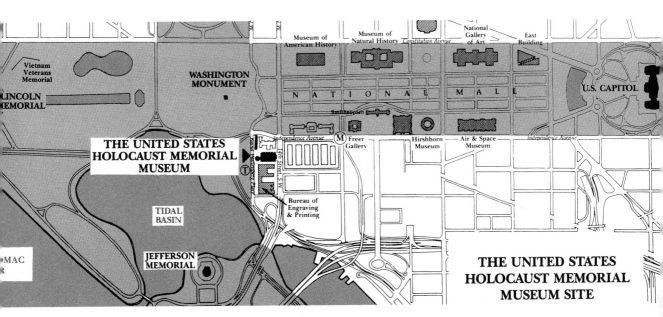

Site plan.

the rise of Nazism, the war years, and, finally, the aftermath of the Holocaust and subsequent efforts to understand it.

The Hall of Witness

The Hall of Witness (7,500 sq ft) is the skylighted core of the building. A three-story arrival, distribution, and circulation space, it is designed to prepare the visitor for the journey that lies ahead. Its forms and ideas are applicable to other memorial-themed museum structures. Important features of the Hall of Witness include the following:

- It is covered by a great twisted skylight, which is dropped at a third-floor level between the museum's brick side walls so that it presses down on the space even as it opens up to the sky.

- The transparent glass admits sheets of unfiltered light that vary with the time of day and season, but are always fragmented by the heavy steel structure through which the light passes.

- From the top of the skylight, a 12-ft-high monitor roof divides the Hall of Witness along a 13-degree diagonal.

- Fifty-seven ft below its peak, the same diagonal cuts through the granite floor as a glass-block incision, filtering light into the lower concourse while shearing the museum experience in two—ordinary museum functions (entry/exit, coatroom, bookstore) on the left, and on the right, extraordinary museum content.

- A glazed two-story bridge spans the Hall of Witness along the west. From the upper level, the bridge overlooks the skylight, its warped and shingled surface visible through the glass, etched with the names of 5,000 obliterated communities.

The Hall of Remembrance

The Hall of Remembrance is a solemn space (6,000 sq ft) with inscriptions carved into limestone walls that encircle an eternal flame. Like the Hall of Witness, it also rises to a skylight, but the glass is translucent, providing a softer, more diffused light.

The message is one of hope for ongoing life as visitors leave the museum, having themselves become witnesses to a never-to-be-repeated past.

Concourse level.
1 Meyerhoff Theater
2 Theater lobby
3 Green room
4 Amphitheater
5 Stairs up to Hall of Witness
6 Education center
7 Classrooms
8 Cinema
9 Elevator lobby
10 Temporary exhibition

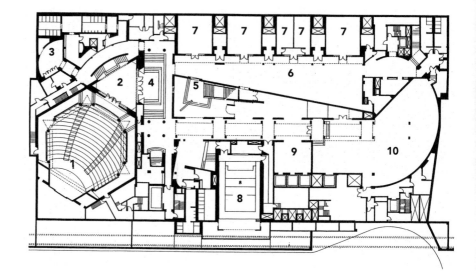

First floor plan.
1 East entry
2 Group entry
3 Stage
4 Hall of Flags
5 Hall of Witness
6 West entry
7 Temporary exhibition
8 Patrons' lounge
9 Coatroom
10 Elevator lobby
11 Bookstore
12 Loading dock

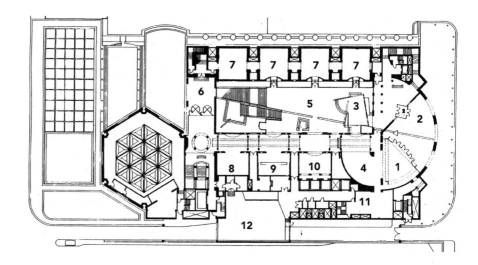

The Hall of Witness features
a three-story atrium. The
Hall's focal point is a
staircase ascending to an
archway resembling the
gates of Birkenau.
Photo: Alan Gilbert

BUILDING SUMMARY

	Area (sq ft)
Hall of Witness	7,500
Hall of Remembrance	6,000
Permanent exhibition	36,000
Temporary exhibitions	8,000
Hall of Learning	3,600
Education/conference center	4,318
Library/archive/research center	16,000
Theater (414 seats)	5,486
Cinema (178 seats)	2,073
Bookstore	1,295
Total	90,272

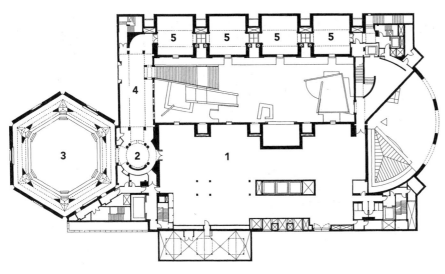

Second floor.
1 *Permanent exhibition*
2 *Antechamber*
3 *Hall of Remembrance*
4 *Gallery of Flags*
5 *Hall of Learning*

Third floor.
1 *Permanent exhibition*
2 *Tower of Life*

Fourth floor.
1 *Permanent exhibition*
2 *Tower of Life*

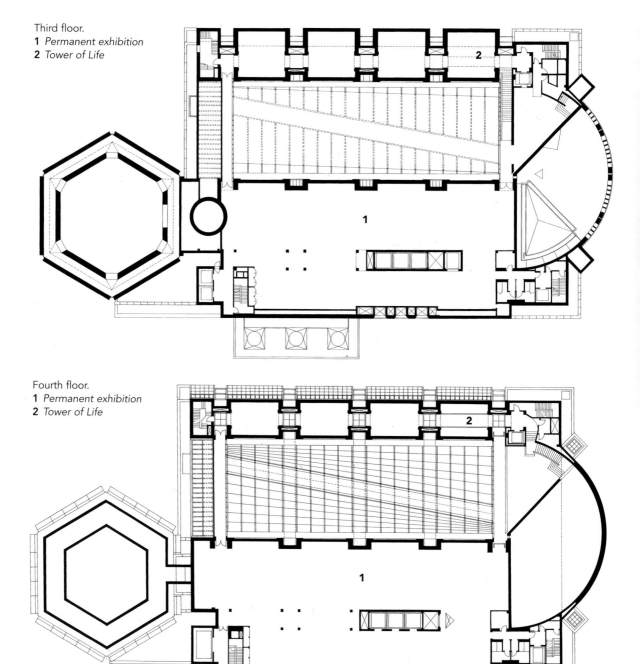

Fifth floor.
1 *Library/archive*
2 *Administration*
3 *Conference room*
4 *Photo archive*
5 *Survivor registry*
6 *Tower of Life*

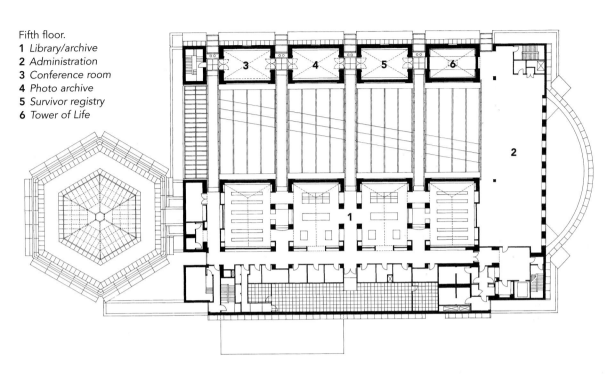

Roof plan.

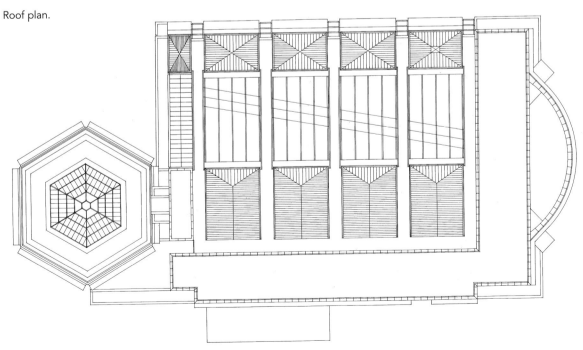

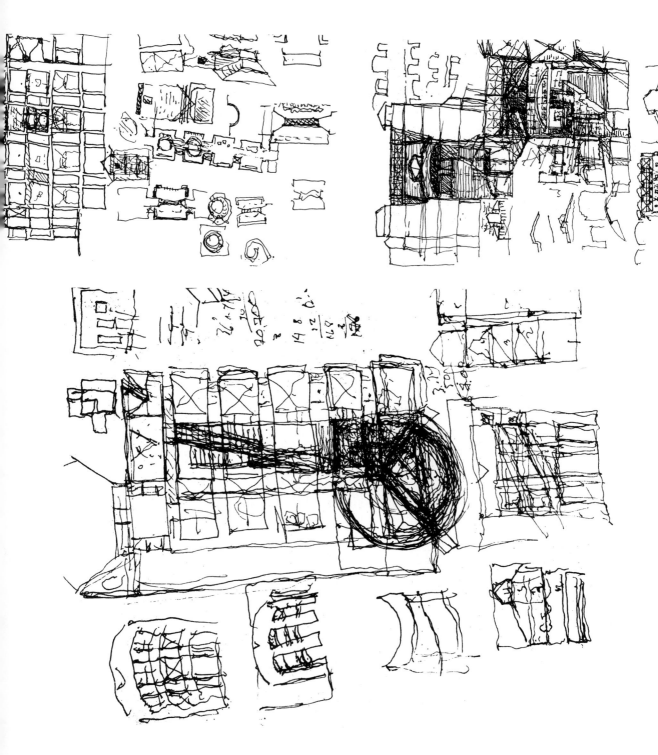

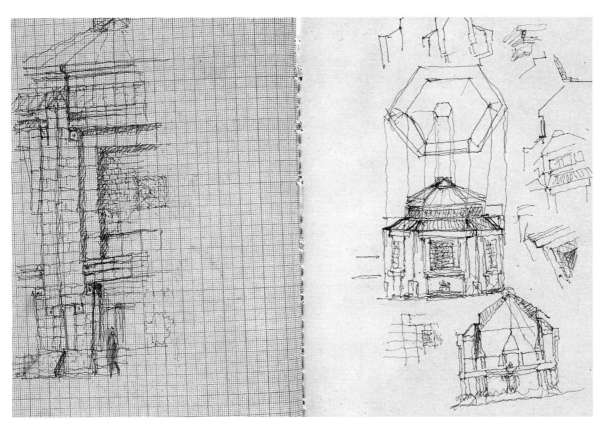

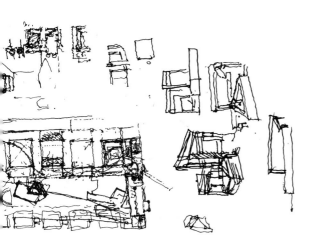

Conceptual drawings
by James Ingo Freed.

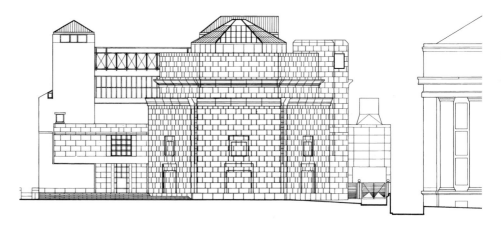

West elevation (Raoul Wallenberg Place).

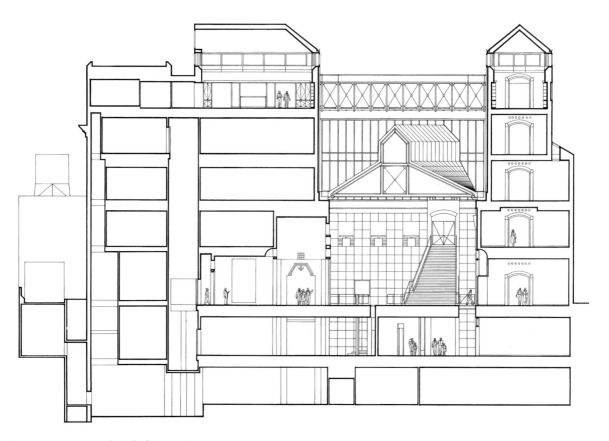

Transverse section with Hall of Remembrance at center.

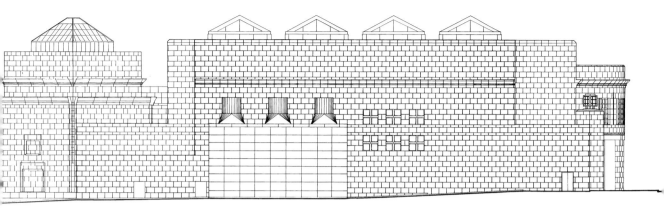

South elevation.

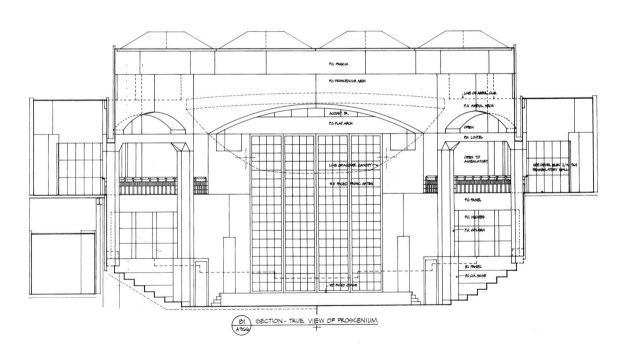

Section through Meyerhoff Theater.

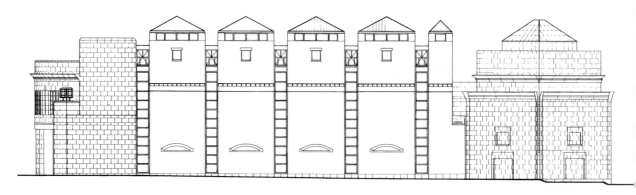

North elevation.

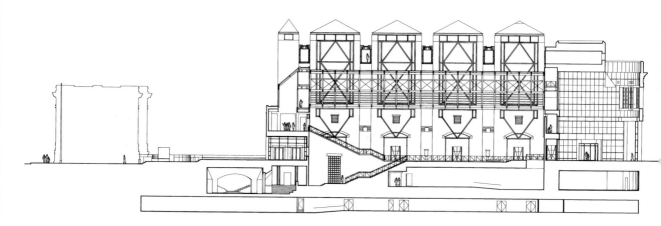

Longitudinal west–east section.

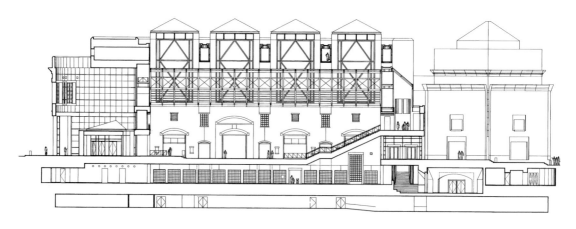

Longitudinal east–west section.

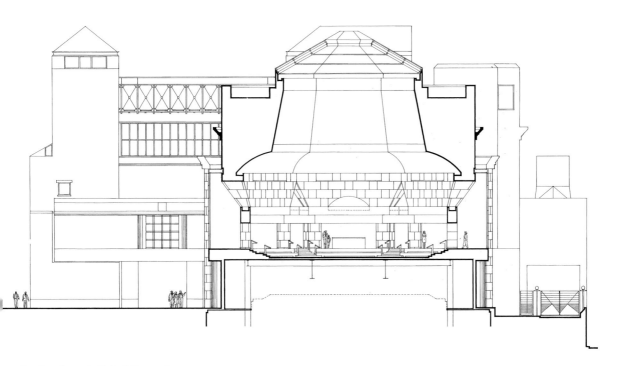

Section through Hall of Remembrance.

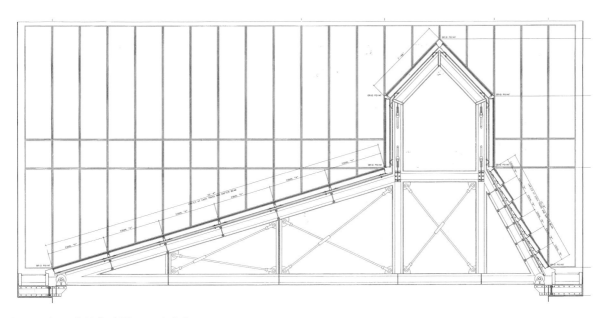

Section through Hall of Witness skylight.

AMERICAN AIR MUSEUM, *Duxford, England*
SIR NORMAN FOSTER & PARTNERS, ARCHITECTS (1997)

Background and Purpose

Foster and Partners were commissioned by the Imperial War Museum, London's premier military defense museum, to develop an innovative way to display its collection of World War II–era U.S. military aircraft, which played such a crucial role in winning the war, as well as earlier and later American military aircraft.

It was also important to protect the fragile aircraft from further environmental damage—many had suffered through long-term exposure to the elements in outdoor locations.

Site

The museum, located in Duxford, East Anglia, was the site of a U.S. air base during the war.

Collection

There are more than 20 authentic U.S. military aircraft in the collection, including the immense B-52 bomber, whose 185-ft wingspan was a key determinant of the shape and form of the plan.

Also included are aircraft from World War I and the Gulf War, many of them still operational as a result of preservation efforts.

Program

The program required:

- That the museum be set within the existing base, with views of the airfield, runways, and beyond

- That the building be a backdrop for the aircraft

Design

The scheme is a huge toruslike (convex, semicircular profile) shape, elliptical in plan. Its single-span vault, the largest of its type in Europe, rises at the structure's fully glazed southeastern elevation to accommodate the tail fin of the B-52 bomber and reduces in height toward the northwest, where it approaches the ground and is partially dug into the landscape.

SIGNIFICANT ISSUES

Program
A World War II history museum emphasizing the U.S. Air Force

Unique design concerns
The display and preservation of fragile authentic war aircraft

Structure system
An exhibit space of enormous size, without columns or other evident supports

Mechanical systems
Emphasis on a stable relative humidity

Lighting design
A complex lighting scheme for illumination of very large aircraft

Wayfinding
A unique entrance providing a self-orienting setting

View from airfield at night.

(text continues on page 182)

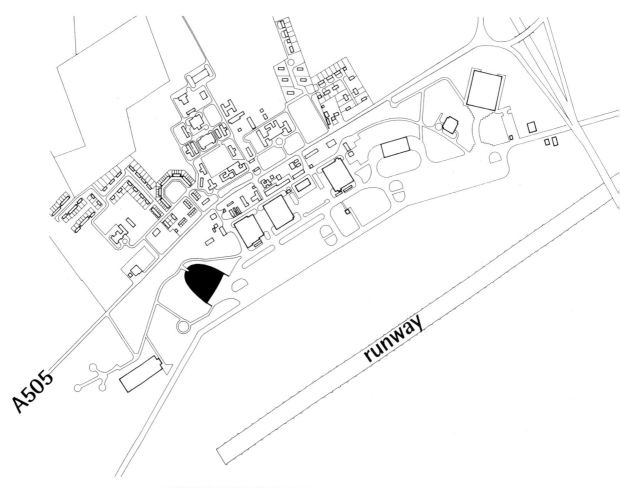

▲ Site plan.

▶ View from airfield at Duxford, England.

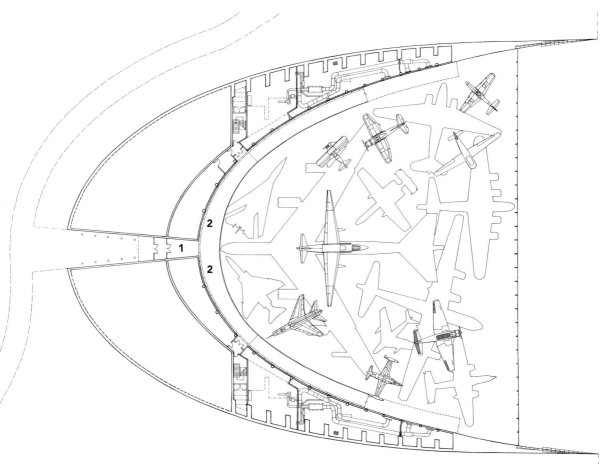

▲ Entry floor plan.
1 *Entry*
2 *Pedestrian ramp to
ground floor*

◄ View of exhibition floor.

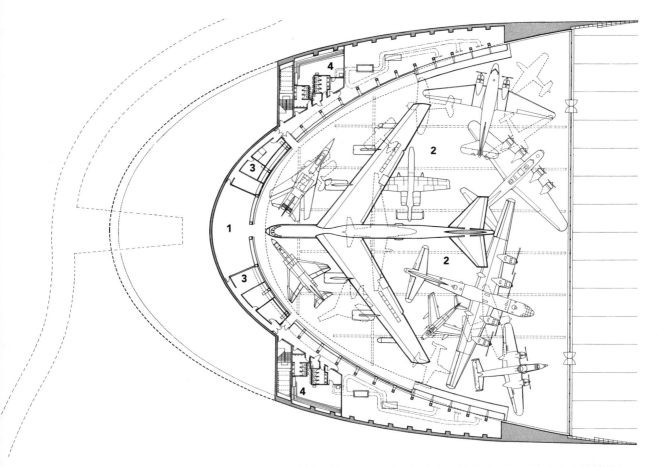

▲ Ground floor plan.
1 *Information/orientation*
2 *Exhibit floor*
3 *Administrative and curatorial offices*
4 *Public toilets*

▶ View of pedestrian entry ramp, overlooking exhibition at ground floor.

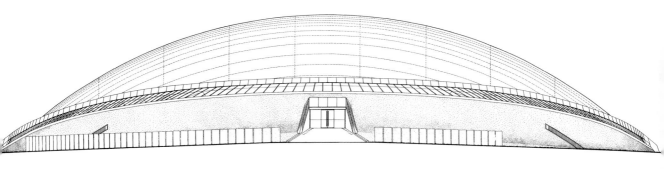

Entry elevation.

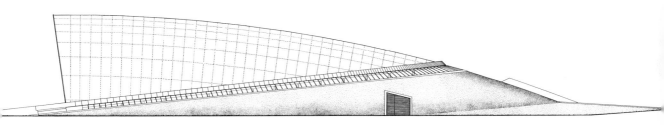

Side elevation.

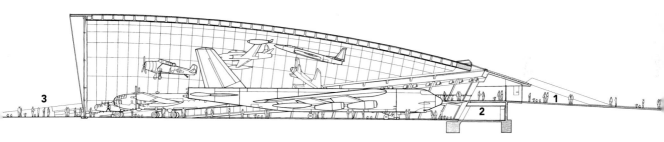

Section.
1 *Entry*
2 *Information/orientation*
3 *Airfield (exterior)*

This unusual roof structure/enclosure spans 295 ft and is 61 ft high. It utilizes a vast assortment of identical precast panels repeated throughout.

Wayfinding

Visitors emerge from a tunnel-like entrance to find themselves midway in the space beneath the concrete shell, facing the nose of the B-52 Stratofortress. Here they can survey a panorama of military craft at every scale, some suspended from the roof, others visible on a floor below.

Mechanical

For purposes of conservation, achieving stable humidity levels were far more important than accommodating variations in temperature. In Britain, where the climate is moderate, huge concrete shell structures can insulate against changes in temperature, thereby removing the need for either air-conditioning or heating.

A fairly simple system achieves a stable relative humidity level of 50 to 55 percent, well below the critical 65 percent level at which aluminum begins to deteriorate. The glazed elevations filter ultraviolet rays, preventing discoloration of the original finish of the aircraft.

Lighting

For lighting the space, the emphasis is on clarity, natural light, and economical environmental and atmospheric systems.

▲ View toward curtain wall and airfield beyond.

▶ Details of curtain-wall assembly, illustrating prefabricated metal tilt-up frame.

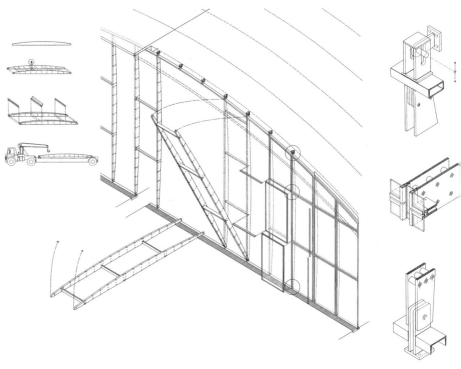

ROUTE 66 MUSEUM, *Clinton, Oklahoma*
RAND ELLIOT, FAIA, OF ELLIOT & ASSOCIATES, ARCHITECT (1995)

Background and Purpose

Completed in 1932, Route 66 is a 2,400-mile two-lane highway, passing through eight states on its way from Chicago, through Oklahoma, and on to Los Angeles. For decades, Route 66 was the road to the promised land—California.

A storytelling museum, mixing scholarship, museology, and pop culture, the Route 66 Museum investigates the impact of this highway on American life.

The museum, operated by the Oklahoma Historical Society, is described by its architect, Rand Elliot, as "a cross between a cheap bar and a motel. We don't have our Whitneys or our Guggenheims out here. What we have is a renegade outlaw kind of tradition—a rich, interesting history—and Route 66 is part of that."

SIGNIFICANT ISSUES

Program
Unorthodox approach to a museum celebrating a highway

Unique design concerns
Installation of full-size Phillips 66 gas station

Interiors
Use of colors, graphics, and architectural features of past decades

Wayfinding
Visually self-orienting—a plan of the museum is not necessary for the visitor

Double-height entrance gallery (WOW Room) utilizes steel trusses typical of bridges along Route 66.
Photo: Hedrich-Blessing

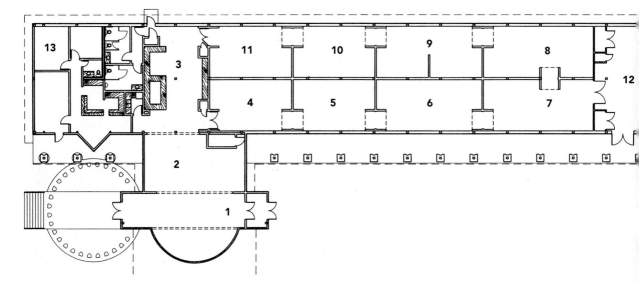

Floor plan.
1 Entry
2 WOW Room (auto showroom with vintage cars).
3 Curio cabinet exhibit
4 Orientation gallery
5 The '20s
6 The '30s
7 The '40s
8 The '50s
9 The '60s
10 The '70s
11 Finale
12 Restoration studio
13 Administration

Site
Site requirements mandated the retention of:

• An adjacent roadside park,

• Three giant elm trees.

Program
The program for the museum had the following objectives.

• To trace the history and culture of Route 66 by examining:
Technological innovations brought about by the automobile and road building
Development of arterial, regional, and national service businesses that changed the economics and landscape of Oklahoma
The effects of these changes on Oklahomans

• To collect materials from television, radio, film, and books dealing with highway transportation in Oklahoma

• To interpret the history of transportation and Route 66 through educational events, activities, and exhibits that increase the general public's curiosity and knowledge

• To promote heritage tourism along the length of historic Route 66

• To seek statewide community appreciation for the Route 66 heritage

• To stimulate preservation of Oklahoma Route 66 properties

The following design criteria emerged from the program:

• Tell the story of Route 66 in chronological order

• Communicate Route 66's sense of adventure

• Emphasize the relationship between personal freedom and automobile travel

• Highlight America's first Main Street

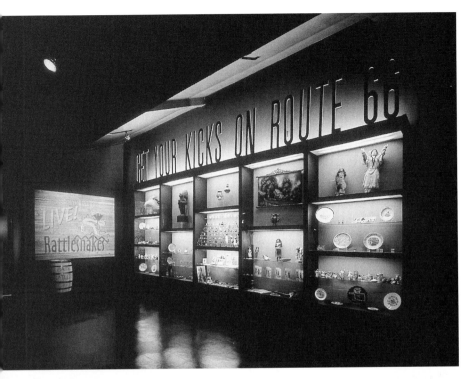

◀ Curio cabinet exhibit is filled with roadside memorabilia associated with Route 66.
Photo: Hedrich-Blessing

▲ Display of Route 66 road marker and automobile license plates of the period.
Photo: Hedrich-Blessing

◀ The diner does not serve food, but evokes Route 66 in the 1950s.
Photo: Hedrich-Blessing

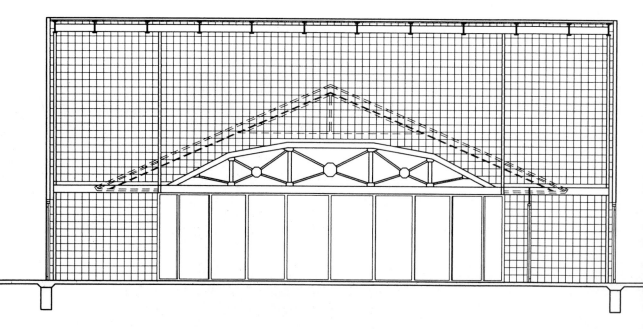

- Incorporate an authentic Phillips 66 gas station to help recall the spirit of the time

Exhibits

An exhibit concept included the following:

- Circulation loop allowing visitors to experience travel along the way

- Organization around automobiles, travel, words and phrases, world events, and popular culture of the period

- Personal travel diary on cassette to guide visitors through the museum

- Installations of artifacts, video images, movies, and memories of the period

A typical exhibit, reminiscent of the 1950s, includes:

- A diner interior, complete with booths, counter, and stools

- A vintage jukebox with 45 rpm records

- A neon arrow sign

- A 1952 Ford sedan

Section through WOW room (entrance and orientation gallery).

McCORD MUSEUM OF CANADIAN HISTORY, *Montreal, Quebec, Canada*

LEMOYNE LAPOINTE MAGNE, ARCHITECTS (1992)

Background

The McCord Museum has the only comprehensive collection of Canadian ethnography in the province of Quebec. One of the most important Amerindian and Inuit collections in Canada, it contains artifacts from Canada's four main cultural divisions of native peoples: Arctic, Eastern Woodlands, Prairies, and the Northwest Coast.

The museum is a storytelling, art, and archeological institution as well as a part of McGill University, where its emphasis is on research and teaching.

Collection

The collection was amassed by Montreal attorney David Ross McCord in the late nineteenth and early twentieth centuries and housed in a limestone palazzo adjacent to McGill University. In the 1980s, the museum expanded to accommodate the growth of the collection and vastly increased its educational and public service activities.

SIGNIFICANT ISSUES

Program
The only comprehensive ethnographic museum in Canada

Unique design concerns
Contemporary expansion near existing limestone palazzo building

Façade of new wing on Rue Victoria.

Program

Formerly restricted by severe overcrowding, it is now possible for the museum to:

- Make the collection and its documentation more accessible to students and scholars

- Take the best possible care of the collection through high standards of preventive conservation

- Support a program of artifact repair and restoration, both in-house and off-site

- Keep a full inventory of the collection and ensure its proper storage

- Develop resident and traveling exhibitions about Canadian history and receive exhibitions from other sources

- Produce educational programs and publications that aid understanding and appreciation of Canadian history

Site plan.
1 *Alliance building*
2 *Existing McCord Building*
3 *New construction*
4 *Adjoining restaurant*

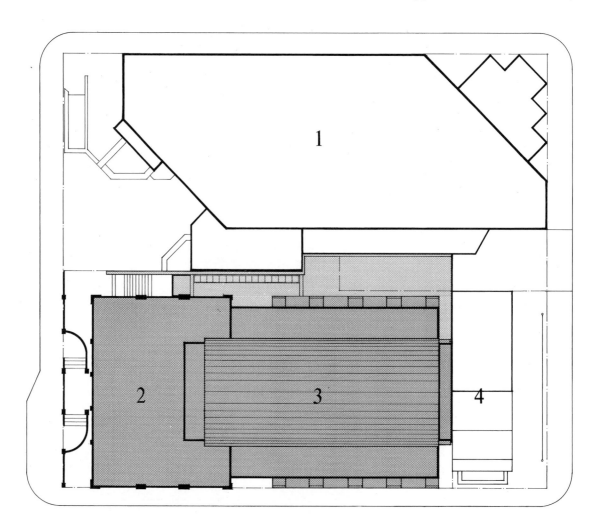

Rendering. *Left:* Existing McCord Museum
designed by Percy E. Nobbs as the McGill
University Student Union in 1906. Home of
the McCord family for more than 20 years.
Right: The new McCord Museum,
completed in 1992. *Background:* The
Alliance building.

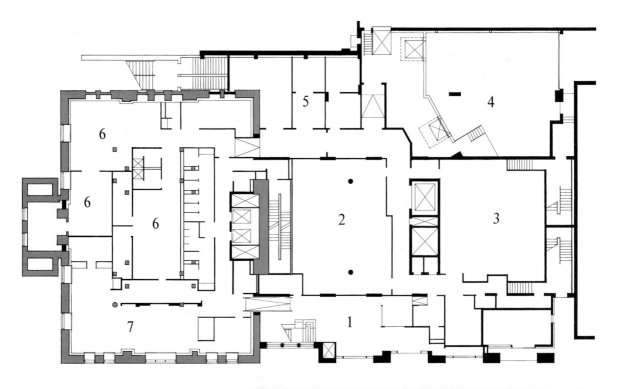

▲ Level 1.
1 *Entry*
2 *Ethnographic collection*
3 *Decorative arts collection*
4 *Loading dock*
5 *Shipping and receiving*
6 *Workshops*
7 *Education*

▶ View of entry foyer on Rue Victoria. Entry provides visual orientation to all floors and suitable display of extremely tall works of art.

PROGRAM SUMMARY

	Area (sq ft)		Area (sq ft)
Public arrival/visitor amenities		Archives	
Lobby, orientation, group reception, coatroom, visitor information center	2,080	Storage	850
		Study area	270
Book/gift shop, storage	1,075	Office and workroom	375
Café and kitchen	750	Artifact research lab	430
Members' lounge	430	Curatorial offices (six curators, clerical and study spaces)	2,300
Security control, first aid station	350		
Education		Registrar (registrar and workroom for condition reports)	870
Children's coat check	350		
Two classrooms	1,720	Conservation	
Student lunchroom	650	Offices	150
Auditorium and projection booth	1,600	Object laboratory	535
Exhibition galleries		Textile laboratory	700
Permanent institutional galleries	6,500	Collection storage	14,000
Special exhibition gallery (including storage area)	3,500	Exhibit preparation	1,000
		Director's office (reception, secretarial, boardroom, etc.)	1,200
Special exhibition gallery	7,800		
Collection galleries		Membership, development, and press	800
Ethnography	420	Operations and administration	2,100
Decorative arts	420	Public programs (includes education, volunteers and docents, continuing education, publications, exhibit design)	7,500
Folk art	420		
Costumes and textiles	700		
Prints and drawings	215	Exhibit development, production and shops (includes exhibition mock-up area)	3,600
Photography	540		
Paintings	420		
Library		Photography studio and darkrooms	1,500
Information catalog	500	Shipping/receiving	
Book stacks	650	Loading dock	500
Reading room	430	Condition report studio	320
Study room	130	Temporary holding	215
Librarian	150	Packing shop	215
		Crate storage	320
		Total	71,550

Note: Square footages are typical of museums of this kind.

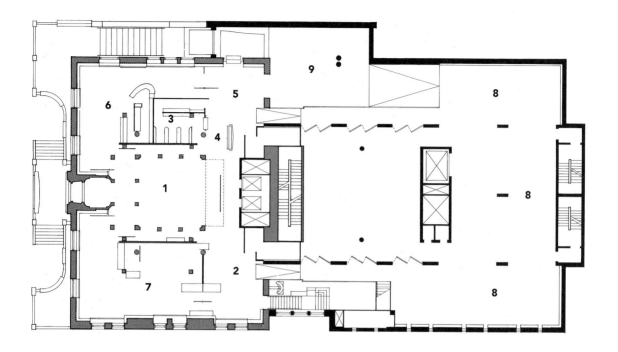

▲ Level 2.
1 Foyer
2 Group visits
3 Coatroom
4 Information
5 Lounge
6 Tearoom/café
7 Bookshop
8 Exhibition galleries
9 Courtyard

▶ Two views of interior court on Level 2, providing visual orientation to exhibition galleries above.

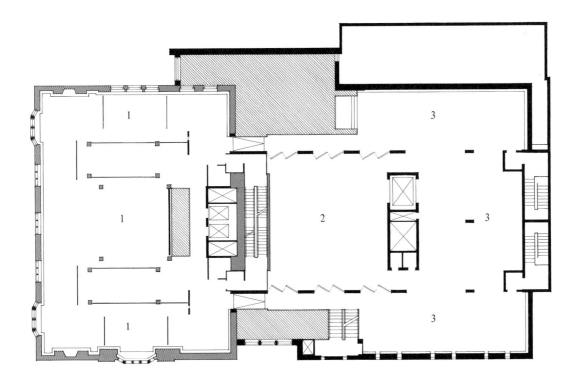

Level 3.
1 *Permanent collection*
2 *Exhibition gallery*
3 *Special exhibition galleries*

▶ View of decorative arts galleries. A simple and direct presentation without period room settings.

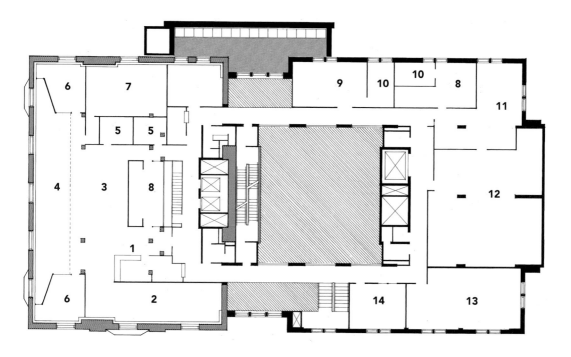

▲ Level 4.
1 Library desk
2 Catalog room
3 Book stacks
4 Reading room
5 Study rooms
6 Office
7 Archival storage
8 Workrooms
9 Photography studio
10 Darkrooms
11 Library consultation
12 Library holding
13 Laboratory
14 Volunteers' room

▶ Typical of small museum libraries. Note study tables adjacent to book stacks.

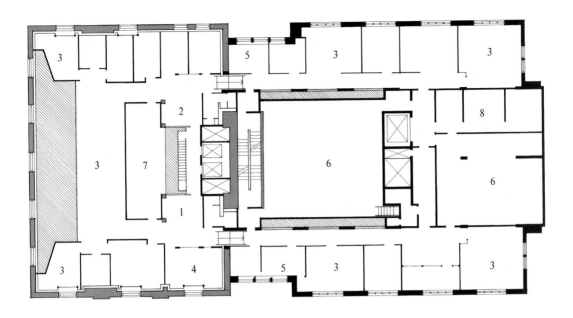

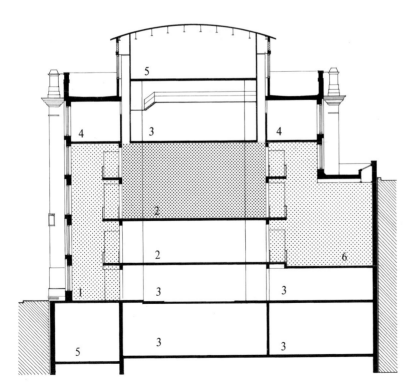

▲ Level 5.
1 *Reception*
2 *Secretary*
3 *Offices*
4 *Staff room*
5 *Meeting room*
6 *Costume and textile collection*
7 *Curatorial laboratory*

◀ Section.
1 *Foyer*
2 *Exhibitions*
3 *Collection storage*
4 *Offices*
5 *Mechanical room*
6 *Interior court*

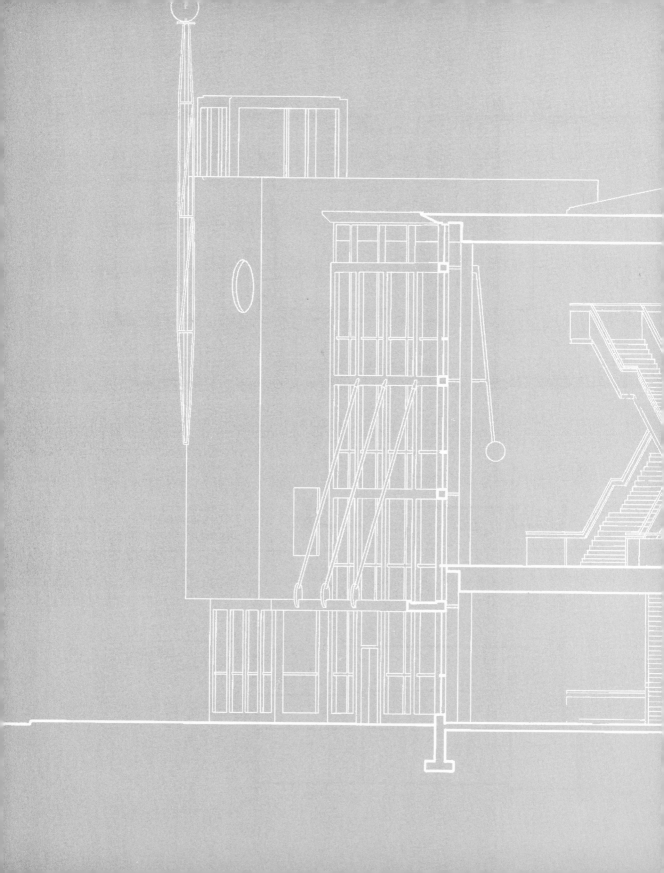

CHILDREN'S AND YOUTH MUSEUMS

CHILDREN'S MUSEUM OF HOUSTON, *Texas*

VENTURI, SCOTT BROWN & ASSOCIATES, ARCHITECTS
JACKSON AND RYAN, ASSOCIATE ARCHITECTS (1992)

Program

The total program of 42,790 sq ft consists of two building elements forming a protected courtyard between them. The museum exhibition building, located on Binz Street, contains flexible space for exhibits and activities in the arts, sciences, and cultural history.

Supporting the main exhibition space, the museum building houses the following:

- A 168-seat auditorium

- Multipurpose classroom spaces

- A science lab

- An art studio

- A video production facility

- A book/gift shop

- Activity space for tots, the youngest children with parents

- A resource center for parents

All activities for children are on the ground floor. All spaces are barrier free and handicapped accessible.

The second building is located at the rear of the property and contains:

- Administration and curatorial offices

- Maintenance and service areas

- Mechanical and electrical equipment

- Exhibition fabrication

- Exhibition design studios

- Storage spaces

Site

A large number of mature pine trees, protected and maintained on the site, were the inspiration for the landscape development of the children's outdoor courtyard. These great trees are the parents of a new forest now growing there.

Plants and trees were chosen to be

- Nonpoisonous to children

- Useful in educating children about varieties of plant life

Design Concerns

The structural design works in concert with the architectural design to achieve

- Open spaces

- Impressively scaled architectural features

- An atmosphere of fun and good spirits

The architects adapted classical symbols for the main façade of the museum

SIGNIFICANT ISSUES

Program
Creation of a children's museum that develops enthusiasm for learning and discovery

Unique design concerns
Adapting classic architectural symbols to a modern structure

Site
A large number of mature trees to be protected

Children's Museum of Houston.

building. The colonnade along Binz Street and the brightly painted caryatids—supporting columns sculptured in the form of women—refer playfully to traditional Greek architecture.

These scultpures are important structural elements. Weighing 600 pounds each, they cover steel-tube columns that hold up the canopy covering the walkway at the school bus entrance.

Because of their human shapes, the columns were configured as an inverted Y, with supports in each leg.

To achieve spaces to be used for multiple functions, the building incorporates both:

- Long-span single-story structural framing and

- Shorter two-story framing

Security and Safety

Because of the museum's location, hurricane-proofing was a necessity. This required a series of inverted V braces to stabilize the building against lateral wind forces. Some of the braces were configured at a severely skewed angle to accommodate wall openings.

Site plan.
1 *Museum building*
2 *Courtyard*
3 *Shop building*

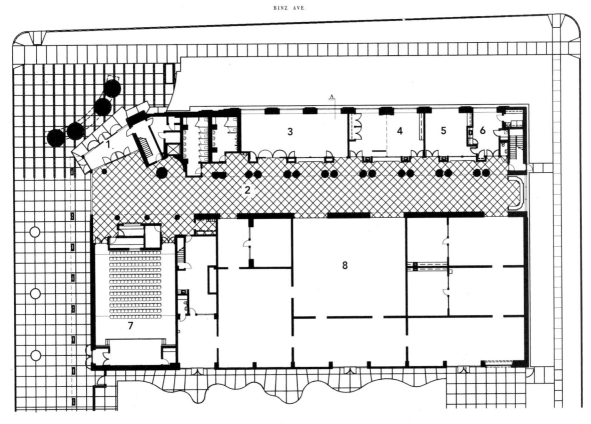

Comfort

The mechanical and electrical systems were designed to give the building support and flexibility. For example, because of the high ceilings of the exhibition gallery, the comfort of the children sitting on the floor in the winter to watch a presentation became a major concern. To solve this problem, return air is removed from the space at the floor perimeter, drawing cold air from the floor and allowing warmer air to take its place.

▲ Ground floor plan.
1 *Entry lobby*
2 *Kid's Hall*
3 *Gift shop*
4 *Classroom*
5 *Celebrations room*
6 *Workroom*
7 *Auditorium*
8 *Galleries*

◄ View of two-story Kid's Hall.

Second floor plan.
1 *Open, upper part of
   entry lobby*
2 *Lobby*
3 *Conference room*
4 *Director*
5 *Work area*
6 *Open, upper part of
   Kid's Hall*

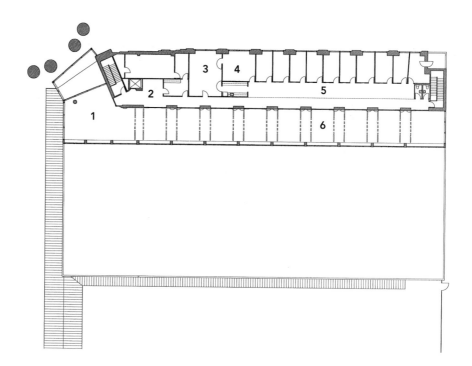

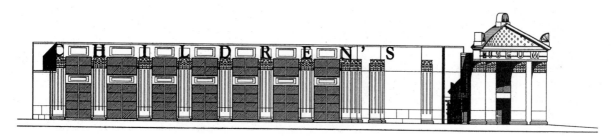

North elevation.

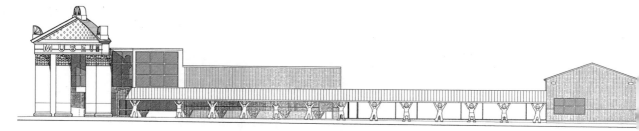

West elevation.

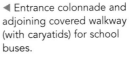

◀ Entrance colonnade and adjoining covered walkway (with caryatids) for school buses.

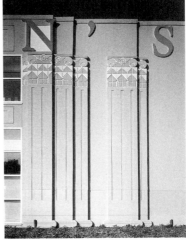

▲ Detail of North elevation.

◀ Entrance lobby.
Photo: Paul Hester

▼ Longitudinal section.
1 *Shop building*
2 *Courtyard*
3 *Exhibitions*
4 *Kid's Hall*
5 *Classroom*
6 *Offices*

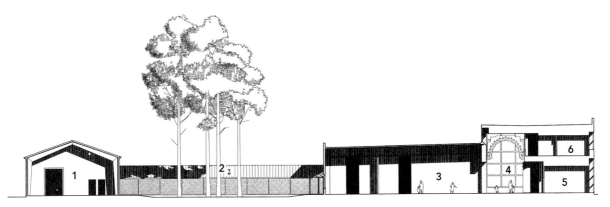

MINNESOTA CHILDREN'S MUSEUM, *St. Paul, Minnesota*
THE ALLIANCE AND JAMES/SNOW ARCHITECTS (1997)

Site

The Minnesota Children's Museum is located in downtown St. Paul, part of an ensemble of cultural institutions known as the Cultural Corridor.

Consisting of three stories and a basement, the building's gross area is 62,000 sq ft. It is bookended by two architectural Goliaths—St. Paul's World Trade Center and the Kohn Pedersen Fox–designed St. Paul Companies' corporate headquarters. Cass Gilbert's Minnesota State Capitol is a few blocks away.

By planting itself visibly at the heart of the city, the museum makes a powerful statement about urban reclamation. Its location becomes part of its persona, aimed at serving children.

Circulation

The museum is organized around a three-story-high glass lobby. Galleries, some of the black-box variety—providing lighting and equipment, but without finished architectural features or decor—are stacked up around the lobby, with an angled staircase that climbs through it. The result is an easy-to-understand floor plan for children and parents alike, as the lobby provides instant orientation to almost any location in the building.

Although many visitors enter on the second floor from a skyway (an enclosed, elevated pedestrian street) that connects through the adjacent World Trade Center, the entry/ticketing lobby is at street level, along with the performance space, the museum store, and administrative offices. This is a typical arrangement of spaces for an urban children's museum.

Galleries

Six galleries, located on the second and third levels, constitute the major program component in the museum, covering about half the program area. An outdoor roof garden on level 3 is near the World Works Gallery.

Each gallery has a single door for both entrance and exit. Because this arrangement reduces the possibility of losing children, parents and teachers can allow them to explore more freely. All fire and safety requirements, of course, are met.

SIGNIFICANT ISSUES

Program
The creation of an innovative urban children's museum

Circulation
How to move large numbers of children from place to place

Site planning
The museum's presence in a commercial area, which raises interesting questions

Wayfinding
Helping young people learn to use a museum

Materials
Use of methods and materials of building that reflect responsibility for the environment

---

View of entrance at night.
Photo: Peter Kerze

Guidelines for Children's Museums

Guidelines for children's museums, developed by the NEA (National Endowment for the Arts) and the University of Southern California, provided these program suggestions for the design of the museum*:

- *First/last impressions.* Arrival and departure represent the first and last impressions of the museum. The process should intrigue, stimulate, and reassure the visitor.

- *Circulation.* Circulation within the building should offer a sense of orientation. Certain areas of exhibits will need to be highly controlled so the actors, storytellers, dancers, and musicians can capture the children's attention.

  Circulation that overlooks the exhibits can provide visitors with a general understanding of the overall sequence through the exhibition space. It can also stimulate curiosity and provide a preview of what is to come.

- *Focal point.* A general focal point within a building can be very helpful for visitors as a place to meet or regroup during visits.

- *Spatial variety.* The use of space in creative, surprising, and unusual ways—spatial variety—enhances

---

*Note: The following is based on guidelines developed by Cohen and McMurtry in "Museums and Children" an unpublished NEA-funded research manuscript (1985) and *The Relocation Feasibility Study* (Los Angeles Children's Museum, University of Southern California, 1987).

architecture and exhibit design and teaches children how to begin to look at objects in space.

- *Outdoor extension.* Whether for exhibits, picnics, or just calm and relaxation, outdoor space is a valuable asset to a children's museum.

- *Preview.* Excitement and interest in the museum can be enhanced if visitors can preview what is going on inside, perhaps by peering into the lobby through large windows when activities are in progress or by watching videos of these activities.

- *Visible backstage.* Some behind-the-scenes activities make excellent exhibits. Areas such as exhibit fabrication (shops), conservation, and offices can be visually open to visitors.

- *Environment.* Building materials and methods of construction can be selected to reflect responsibility for the environment, respect for cultural diversity, and accommodation for those with disabilities or handicaps.

- *Safety concerns:*
  Stairs and railings should be appropriately sized.
  Doors should be easy to open and close.
  Lighting should highlight changes in elevation.
  Flooring and wall materials should be impact absorbing.
  Sharp corners and edges should be avoided.
  Emergency lighting and signage should articulate exit pathways.

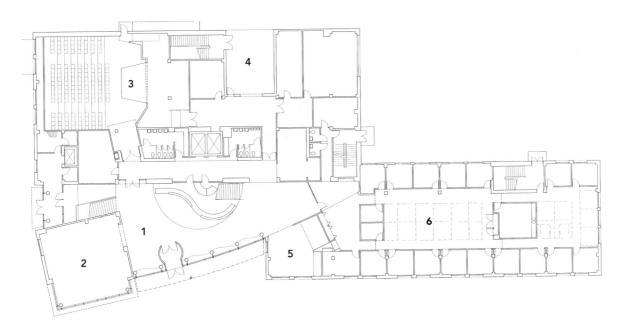

▲ Ground floor plan.
1 *Entry lobby*
2 *Museum store*
3 *Auditorium*
4 *Service entrance*
5 *Lunchroom*
6 *Administration offices*

◀ Glazed core of museum's entrance lobby overlooks West Seventh Street in urban St. Paul.
Photo: Peter Kerze

MINNESOTA CHILDREN'S MUSEUM PROGRAM

Visitor Service	Area (sq ft)
Lobby and vestibule	1,950
Information and admissions	100
Visitor service office	320
Museum store	
Sales area	1,000
Manager's office	120
Workroom	150
Storage	150
Support spaces	
Coat check	900
Caterer's kitchen	150
Vending machines	50
Boys' and girls' restrooms	600
Unisex toilet	50
Diaper changing/nursing area	50
Visitor Service total:	5,590

Galleries	
Exhibit galleries	
World of Wonder	4,500
Earth World	5,500
World Works	5,230
One World	5,225
Habitot (children 6 mos.–2 yrs.)	1,750
Changing World	2,500
Subtotal	24,705

Gallery programs	Area (sq ft)
Gallery classroom	500
Gallery classroom	500
Classroom storage	50
Table and chair storage	100
Subtotal	1,150
Gallery support	
Four unisex toilets	160
Housekeeping and storage	160
Subtotal	320
Gallery total:	26,175

Public Programs	
Performance space	2,500
Central room	120
Offstage storage	300
Activity center	1,000
Workroom and storage	200
Public Programs total:	4,120

Offices	
Exhibits office	
Exhibits director	120
Developer/evaluator	240
Technician	120
Clerical	80
Workroom	300
Subtotal	860

Note: Program details provided by and used with the permission of the Minnesota Children's Museum. These areas are typical for large city children's museums.

	Area (sq ft)
Program offices	
Program director	120
Museum educators	160
Project coordinators	160
Clerical	80
Visitors service manager	80
Volunteers	240
Subtotal	840
Development offices	
Director	120
Development associate	240
Marketing manager	120
Marketing associate	160
Clerical	300
Workroom	280
Subtotal	1,220
Administrative offices	
Finance and administrative director	120
Accounting	120
Human resources	120
Clerical	140
Subtotal	500
Executive offices	
Executive director	180
Executive assistant	80
Vice president of programs	120
Vice president for administration	120
Subtotal	500

	Area (sq ft)
Office support spaces	
Conference room	800
Library	150
Reception and waiting	220
Miscellaneous/toilets, mailroom, office supplies, copy room	360
Subtotal	1,530
Office total:	5,450

Exhibit Fabrication

Wood shop	3,000
Metal Shop	400
Finishing room	1,000
Shop storage	1,000
Office and toilet	170
Exhibit Fabrication total:	5,570

Staff Facilities

Staff kitchen	250
Kitchen	50
Lockers, showers, and toilets	280
Staff Facilities total:	580

Building Operations

Shipping, loading dock, receiving, trash disposal	3,000
General storage	500
Fire and security control	80
Maintenance shop and janitor rooms	360
Building Operations total:	3,940

CHILDREN'S AND YOUTH MUSEUMS

Second floor plan.
1 *Lobby*
2 *Boardroom*
3 *"Skyway" elevated
   pedestrian street*
4 *Exhibition space*
5 *Classroom*

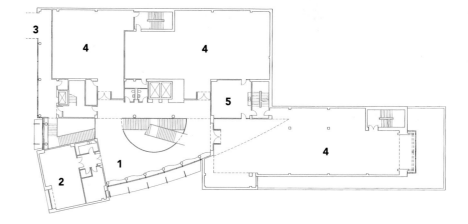

Third floor plan.
1 *Early childhood exhibits*
2 *Parenting support*
3 *Roof garden*
4 *Exhibition space*
5 *Classroom*

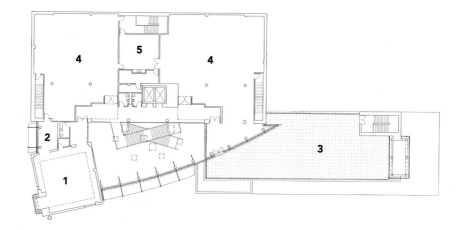

Basement.
1 *Exhibition fabrication
   shops; maintenance and
   operation*

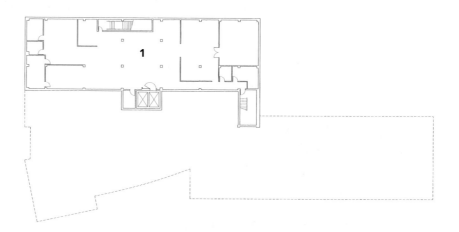

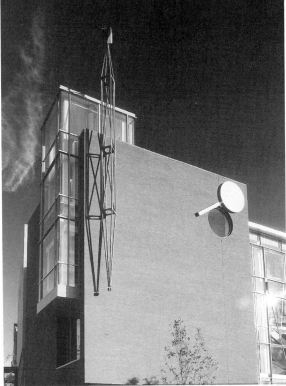

◄ Aluminum "magnifying glass" is designed to be motorized and rotate over opening, creating crescent moon window.
Photo: Don F. Wong

◄ Galleries on the second and third floors surround the central open space and stair, where performers and museum staff greet children.
Photo: George Heinrich

▲ Vincent James–designed lobby's colorful mural and "lollipop" light fixtures. Stair incorporates two railings to accommodate small and smaller people.
Photo: Don F. Wong

CHILDREN'S AND YOUTH MUSEUMS

North–South section.
1 *Entrance lobby*
2 *Service entrance*
3 *Exhibition fabrication shops; maintenance and operation*
4 *One World exhibition*
5 *Earth World gallery*

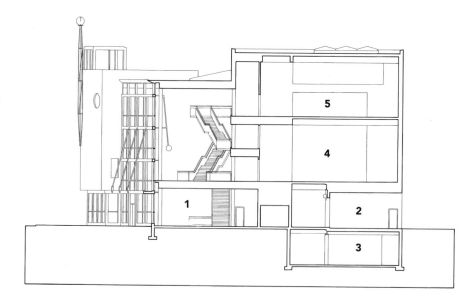

▶ Saint Peter elevation.

▼ West Seventh elevation.

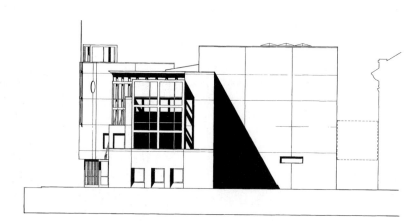

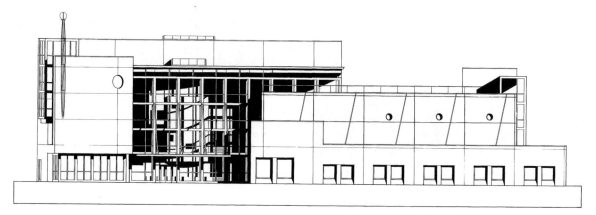

SCIENCE
AND
NATURAL
HISTORY
MUSEUMS

FREDERICK PHINEAS AND SANDRA PRIEST ROSE CENTER FOR EARTH AND SPACE, *New York, New York*

POLSHEK PARTNERSHIP, ARCHITECTS (2000)

The Rose Center is a 334,000 sq ft, seven-floor exhibition and research facility within the American Museum of Natural History. It houses:

- The Hayden Planetarium

- The Lewis B. and Dorothy Cullman Hall of the Universe

- The David S. and Ruth L. Gottesman Hall of Planet Earth

The Hayden Planetarium

The centerpiece of the facility is an 87-ft sphere that appears to float within a glass-walled cube 95 ft high.

The Hayden Planetarium is housed in the upper half of the sphere and contains the following:

- The state-of-the-art Space Theater, whose technologies include a customized Zeiss Star Projector (MKIX), the most advanced in the world, offering hyperrealistic views of the solar system

- The Digital Dome System, which provides a scientifically accurate virtual recreation of our galaxy and what lies beyond, based on data from NASA (the National Aeronautics and Space Administration), the European Space Agency's Hipparcos database of more than 100,000 stars, and a statistical database of more than 2 billion stars developed by the American Museum of Natural History

The new planetarium uses visualization tools, including:

- Silicon Graphics

- Onyx 2

- Infinite Reality 2

- Trimension display and integration technology

The lower half of the sphere houses:

- The Big Bang Theater, a multisensory recreation of the first moments of the universe

- The Harriet and Robert Heilbrunn Cosmic Pathway, a sloping walkway through 13 billion years of cosmic evolution

SIGNIFICANT ISSUES
Program   The most technologically advanced planetarium in the world
Circulation   Bringing new facilities to an older museum
Unique design concerns   How to anticipate and integrate fast-changing scientific discoveries into the new center
Structure system   A giant column-free sphere for the planetarium theater
Special equipment   Unique assemblage of equipment for projection

Frederick Phineas and Sandra Priest Rose Center for Earth and Space

View from West 81st Street.
Photo: American Museum of
Natural History

The Lewis B. and Dorothy Cullman Hall of the Universe

The features of this hall are as follows:

- The Universe Zone illustrates the force of gravity and the warping of space and time.

- The Galaxies Zone demonstrates the collision of two galaxies.

- The Stars Zone tells about the explosion of a star into a supernova.

- The Planet Zone depicts the William Meteorite, a relic of the solar system weighing 15½ tons.

The David S. and Ruth L. Gottesman Hall of Planet Earth

This 8,900 sq ft hall, nicknamed HOPE, focuses on Earth and its geologic history. Built around rock samples and models of geographic sites from all over the world, together with state-of-the-art computer equipment and video displays, it asks questions about our planet's existence and dynamic processes. Featured are:

- 168 samples and 11 full-scale models of locales such as:
  Mount Vesuvius
  the Grand Canyon
  the Swiss Alps

- Towering sulfide chimneys from the Pacific Ocean floor

- A replica of a 115,000-year-old ice core sample from Greenland

- A satellite view of Earth

- An Earth Event Wall, presenting in-depth reports of atmospheric events such as earthquakes and volcanos as they happen

Lower level plan.
1 *American Museum of Natural History*
2 *Cullman Hall of the Universe*
3 *Parking*

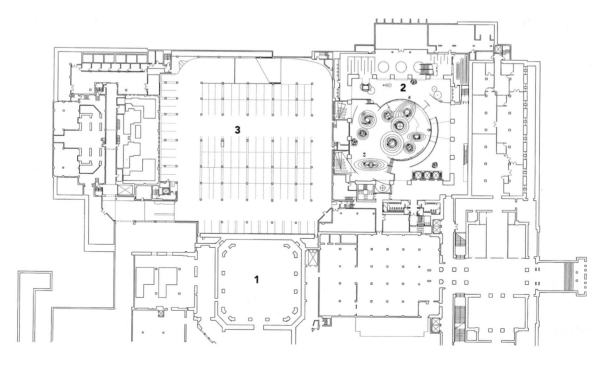

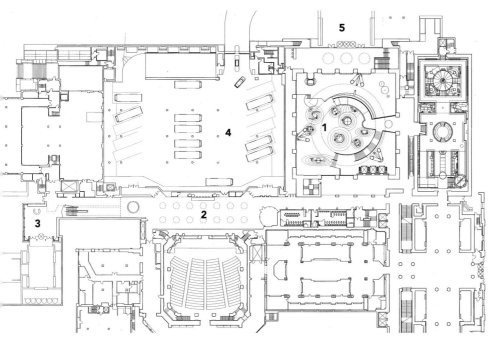

First floor plan.
1 *Hall of the Universe*
2 *Gallery*
3 *Columbus Avenue entrance*
4 *Parking*
5 *Park entrance*

▲ Scales of the Universe exhibit.
Photo: American Museum of Natural History

◄ Walkway surrounding Planetarium enclosure with view of Central Park.
Photo: Polshek Partnership

▼ Gallery below Planetarium Sphere.
Photo: American Museum of Natural History

▲ View of Ecosphere exhibit.
Photo: American Museum of Natural History

▲ Interior view of Planetarium.
Photo: Polshek Partnership

Frederick Phineas and Sandra Priest Rose Center for Earth and Space

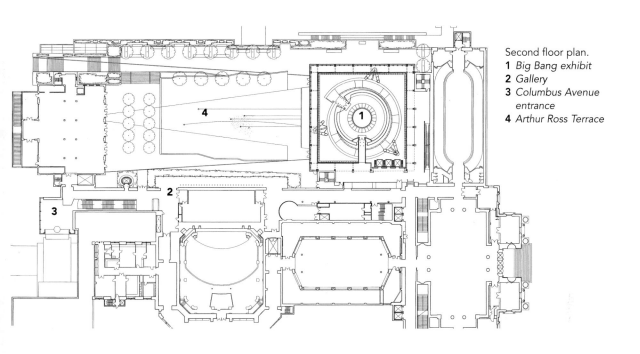

Second floor plan.
1 *Big Bang exhibit*
2 *Gallery*
3 *Columbus Avenue entrance*
4 *Arthur Ross Terrace*

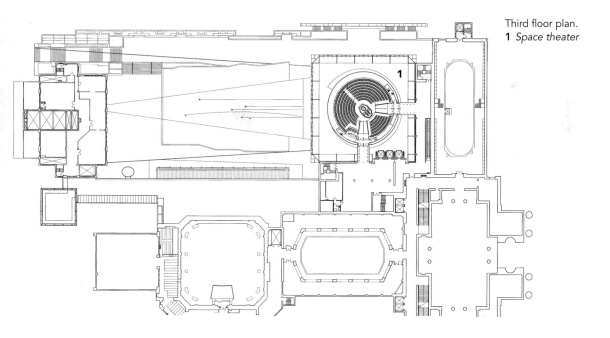

Third floor plan.
1 *Space theater*

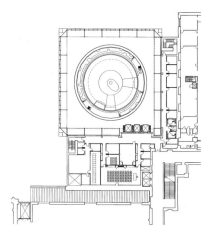

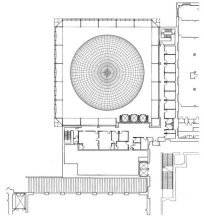

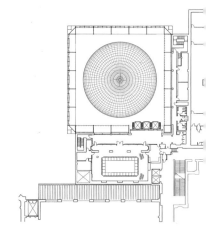

Fourth floor.

Fifth floor.

Sixth floor.

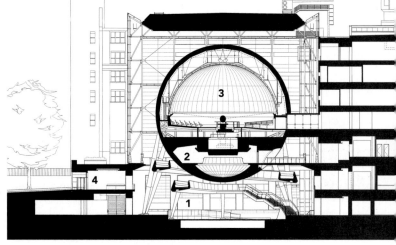

▲ Section through center.
1 Cullman Hall of the Universe
2 Big Bang exhibit
3 Hayden Planetarium
4 Park entrance

◄ View of Planetarium structure during construction.
Photo: Polshek Partnership

ARIZONA SCIENCE CENTER, *Phoenix, Arizona*
ANTOINE PREDOCK, ARCHITECT (1997)

Program
The 69,800 sq ft center consists of the following:

- Exhibition space
- A theater
- A planetarium
- Educational and support facilities

Site
The Science Center is situated along a major traffic route leading into the center of Phoenix; there are residences to the east, a convention center to the west, relocated historic houses to the north, and warehouses to the south. Also close by are a civic center, a symphony hall, and a history museum.

   Parking is available off-site. The museum does not provide parking.

SIGNIFICANT ISSUES

Program
A new science museum and planetarium

Unique design concerns
A modern structure adjoining a historic district

Special equipment
Use of extensive multimedia projection in the planetarium

Entrance plaza approach.
Photo: Timothy Hursley

PRINCIPAL SPACES

	Area (sq ft)			Area (sq ft)

Level 1

Two outdoor garden courts, suitable for receptions and other functions	5,400
Entrance lobby and Great Hall for receptions of up to 500 persons	4,400
Dorrance Planetarium, with:	
206 seats	
A 60 ft diameter dome	
Computer-driven multimedia projection equipment	
	2,900
Irene P. Flinn Theater, with:	
285 seats	
A giant screen	
An IWERKS 870 projector	
	5,100
Four classrooms, occupancy 20 to 30 per room	3,000
All About You Gallery, a hands-on exhibit revealing the workings of the human body and mind (nearby play space available for very young children)	10,000
Special exhibition gallery	4,000
Book/gift shop	2,000

Level 2

Kresge Gallery, with exhibits on:	
Anthropology	
Ant colonies	
The Internet	
An amateur radio station	
	4,000
Administrative, education, and curatorial offices	10,000

Level 3

The World Around You Gallery, with exhibits on:	
Arizona themes	
Geology	
Aerospace	
the Sun	
Air-conditioning a house	
Electricity	
Laser light	
Prospecting for minerals	
	10,000
America West Gallery, with exhibits on:	
Deciphering puzzles	
Gyroscopes	
Molecules in action	
Liquid nitrogen	
	2,000

Level 4

The Peak Gallery, with temporary exhibits on relationships between science, nature, art, and photography	1,000
Outdoor terraces, suitable for receptions and other events are:	
Upper Terrace (third level)	1,200
Canyon Terrace (third level)	3,000
Star Terrace	1,800
Total	69,800

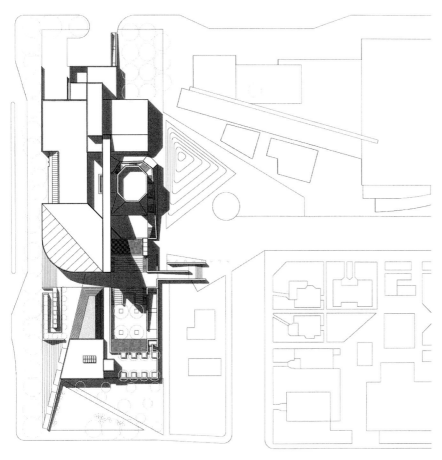

Site plan.

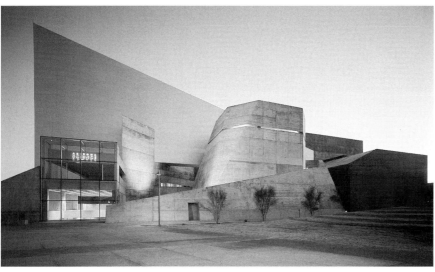

View at night.
Photo: Timothy Hursley

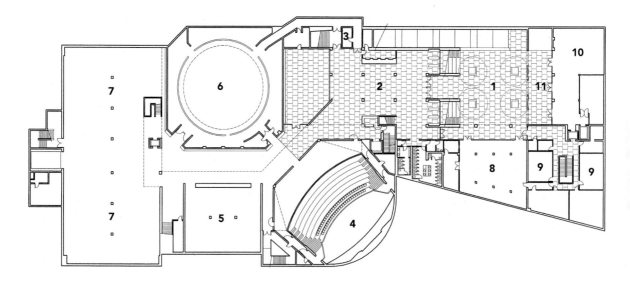

▲ Entry level plan.
1 Entry court
2 Lobby
3 Security
4 Film theater
5 Demonstration theater
6 Planetarium
7 Exhibitions
8 Museum store
9 Administration
10 Food service
11 Outdoor dining

▶ Entry lobby.
Photo: Timothy Hursley

▼ Section.
1 Entry court
2 Lobby
3 Planetarium
4 Exhibitions
5 Food service

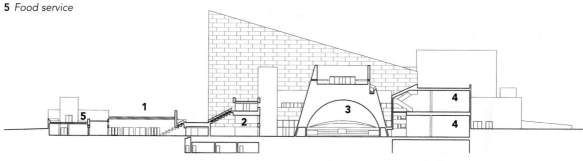

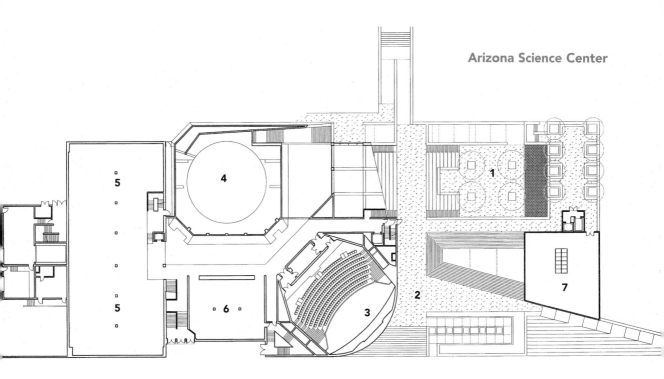

▲ Plan of street approach and plaza level.
1 *Entry court*
2 *Approach plaza*
3 *Upper film theater*
4 *Upper Planetarium*
5 *Exhibitions*
6 *Upper demonstration theater*
7 *Administration*

◄ View of Exhibition area.
Photo: Timothy Hursley

SPECIALIZED MUSEUMS AND GALLERIES

CENTRAL PARK WILDLIFE CENTER AND WILDLIFE GALLERY, *New York, New York*
KEVIN ROCHE JOHN DINKELOO AND ASSOCIATES, ARCHITECTS (1988)

This zoo is an outstanding example of the safari concept that is beginning to dominate zoo planning.

Background
Built by the Federal Works Progress Administration (WPA) during the Great Depression of the 1930s, the original zoo presented penned-up animals to a curious public.

In the 1980s, the Central Park Zoo was recreated as the Central Park Wildlife Center and Wildlife Gallery. In this completely new facility, the only horticultural feature of the original zoo that has been retained and restored is the formal garden in the center. Around that garden is a trellised, glass-covered arcade, which provides sheltered visitor connections to all the exhibits.

SIGNIFICANT ISSUES

Program
Modernization of a large, older urban zoo

Circulation
To simulate a walk through animals' natural habitats

Unique design concerns
Retention of certain of the zoo's original design features

Materials
Careful adherence to natural materials found in animals' native environments

Design
Key design elements of the new Wildlife Center include the following:

• The safari concept is used in a simulated visit to the animals' natural habitats, showing them living in conditions that duplicate their native environments as closely as possible. Observers are kept at a safe distance by natural barriers such as streams or gullies.

• Three major exhibit areas are the tropic zone, the temperate zone, and the polar zone.

• The potentially obtrusive mass of the structures is reduced to a background of neutral brick walls by a trellised arcade made of granite, wood, and glass.

• New construction echoes the materials and forms of the original WPA structures.

• An exhibition and educational gallery and book/gift shop are located in two of the restored and refurbished original buildings.

• Where natural habitats require a change of climate, it is provided artificially in a sealed environment with sophisticated mechanical/electrical systems. Visitors observe these exhibits through glass.

• Trees on the site were carefully preserved, and the zoo's WPA-commissioned animal sculptures have been placed in prominent locations throughout the Wildlife Center.

Aerial view (looking west) of
Central Park Zoo, with New
York skyline in background.

SPECIALIZED MUSEUMS AND GALLERIES

Site Plan

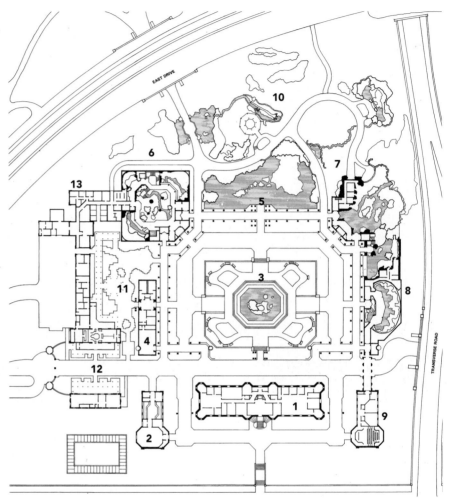

Aerial view (looking north) of zoo.

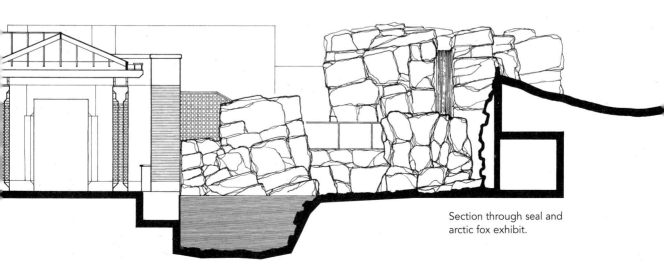

Section through seal and arctic fox exhibit.

▲ Passage and observation terrace at temperate territory zone.

▶ View of formal garden and sea lion exhibits.

Rendering and photo of wood and brick trellis passages connecting freestanding zoo structures.

BEYELER FOUNDATION MUSEUM, *Basel, Switzerland*

RENZO PIANO BUILDING WORKSHOP, ARCHITECT (1997)

Background and Purpose

Renzo Piano responded to the assignment by saying, "A museum must attempt to reflect the quality of the collection and define its relationship with the outside world."

The Beyeler Foundation Museum is typical of a growing number of relatively small museums devoted to limited collections.

Other examples include the following:

- Philip Johnson's Painting Gallery in New Canaan, Connecticut

- The Saatchi Collection Gallery by architect Max Gordon in London

- The Goetz Collection by Herzog and de Meuron in Munich, Germany

Collection

The Beyeler collection consists of 160 works by 33 artists and represents a comprehensive overview of classical modern art. It includes works of Paul Cézanne, Vincent van Gogh, Piet

Detail of elevation.
Photo: M. Denance

SIGNIFICANT ISSUES

Program
Museum for small, high-quality art collection

Site planning
Compatibility with site in a suburban public park

Lighting design
An original roof system allowing an abundance of natural light

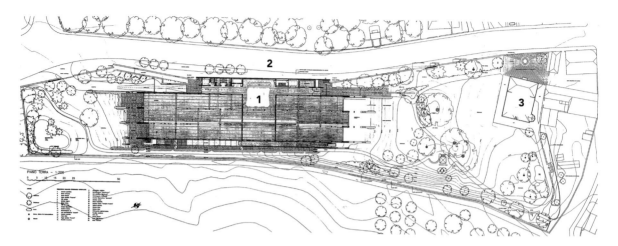

Site plan.
1 *Beyeler Foundation Museum*
2 *Route of highway in Riehen, a suburb of Basel, Switzerland*
3 *Villa Berower, existing structure to be used as offices, library, and museum restaurant*

Aerial view of museum site.
Photo: M. Denance

Mondrian, Pablo Picasso, Wassily Kandinsky, Paul Klee, Mark Rothko, Barnett Newman, and Anselm Kiefer.

Two or three yearly changing or temporary exhibitions are presented, with works from various museum collections.

Site
The site is a nineteenth-century park in a suburb of Basel. The new building, reserved primarily to exhibit art, occupies a narrow plot situated between a busy connecting road and government-protected agricultural land.

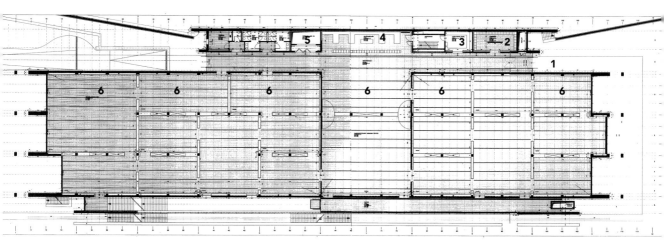

An existing structure on the property, the historic Villa Berower, houses:

- Curatorial and administrative offices

- A library

- A restaurant for visitors

Design

The form of the one-story structure is simple.

- Four parallel load-bearing walls (each 394 ft long, 23 ft apart) divide the interior into a series of galleries and support a glass roof.

- A fifth, windowless wall encloses:
  The bookshop
  Toilets
  Coatrooms
  Miscellaneous nongallery spaces.

- Within a sixth wall, a Winter Garden provides a pleasant outdoor retreat.

- A basement level, entered through the Winter Garden, houses a temporary exhibition gallery.

Wayfinding

Galleries are arranged for visitors to create their own paths through the building.

Lighting Design

Abundant natural light comes from an original roof system made entirely of glass and steel. Resting on the internal load-bearing walls and additional exterior supports, the 43,000 sq ft of glass roof is 26 ft above the floor. This roof allows light to filter into the gallery spaces in an almost natural state. When daylight is insufficient, artificial light sources are used.

Integrated within the glass and steel roof is a 5.25 ft space for mechanical equipment, electronically controlled louvers, and incandescent light (used only at night). The double-glazed outer layer of roof construction incorporates a laminate that provides ultraviolet filtration.

Above the roof is a tilted *brise-soleil*, an arrangement of horizontal glass fins coated to make them partially opaque. The roof system also provides space for the future production of solar energy.

Plan.
1 *Entry*
2 *Coat check*
3 *Admissions*
4 *Book shop*
5 *Freight elevator*
6 *Galleries*

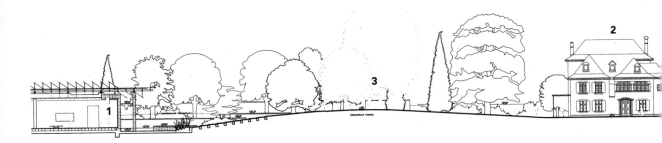

▲ Section through site.
1 *Beyeler Museum*
2 *Villa Berower (offices,
   library, and restaurant)*
3 *Landscape garden*

▶ View of perimeter gallery.
Photo: M. Denance

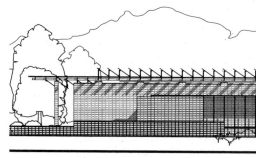

This, one of the most original modern concepts for gallery illumination, is an important example of innovative design.

Footcandle values of the galleries are regulated in two ways:

- Louvers within the loft spaces are automatically controlled in response to inputs from externally mounted photocells.

- To maintain proper electric lighting, light levels in galleries are automatically measured every 15 minutes and can be examined historically.

◀ View of interior gallery.
Photo: M. Denance

▼ Elevation.

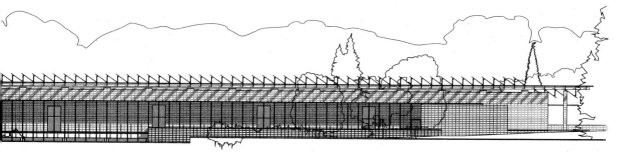

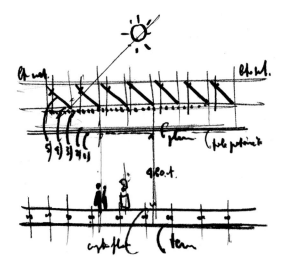

Conceptual sketch by Renzo Piano of glass roof and lighting system.

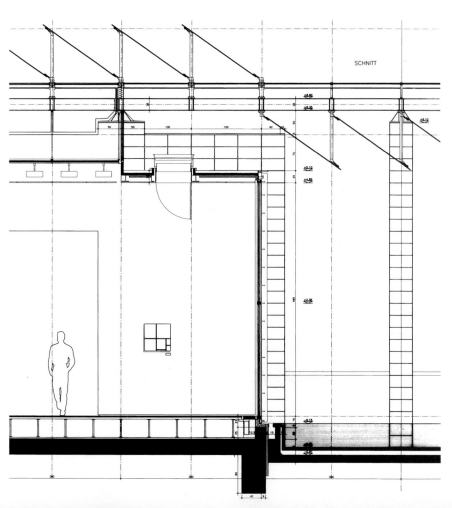

Longitudinal wall section. Note exterior placement of rooftop tilted *brise-soleils*, whose glass panels are partially silk-screened to make them opaque.

Detail of glass *brise-soleil*.
Photo: M. Denance

Detail of glass roof system.
Photo: M. Denance

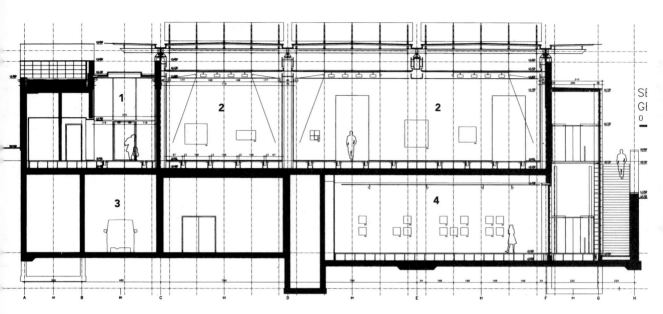

▲ Transverse section.
1 *Entry lobby*
2 *Galleries*
3 *Basement service*
entrance
4 *Workshop*

▶ Longitudinal section
through *brise-soleil*.

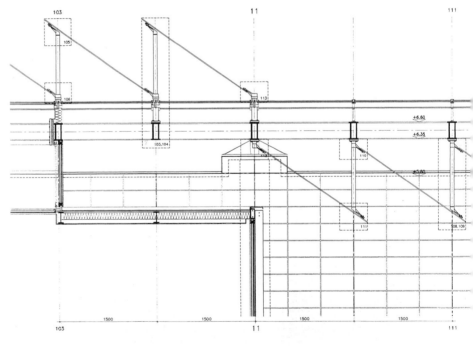

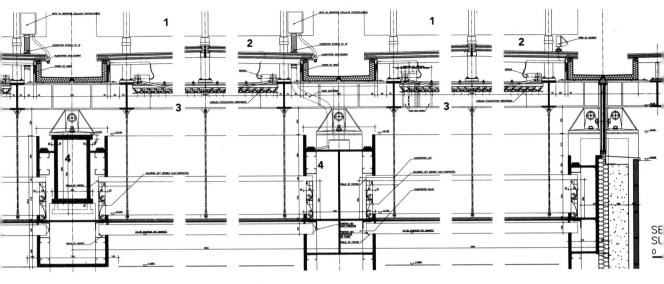

▲ Transverse section through roof.
1 *Exterior* brise-soleil *glass panels*
2 *Glass roof*
3 *Electronically controlled louvers*
4 *HVAC supply duct*

◀ Detail of glass roof system.
Photo: M. Denance

JACK AND BELLE LINSKY GALLERIES, METROPOLITAN MUSEUM OF ART, *New York, New York*

KUPIECKOUTSOMITIS ARCHITECTS, HENRI SAMUEL CONSULTING DESIGNER (1985)

Purpose

This complex of seven galleries houses an historic ensemble of French furniture, Italian paintings, Renaissance jewelry, medieval bronzes, enamels, porcelains, and much more—brought together under the best possible museological conditions and using the most modern techniques of:

- Display

- Security

- Presentation

Site

Located adjacent to the museum's Medieval sculpture hall, the Linsky Galleries are almost residential in scale, with the largest space only 27 by 30 ft

SIGNIFICANT ISSUES

Unique design concerns
An historically correct setting for an eccentric collection

Interior issues
Complex details and finishes not readily available today

Renovation
The alteration of galleries within an existing historic landmark

Variety of objects
Working with diverse elements and materials of many shapes and sizes

Concealed technology
Innovative introduction of mechanical features

and with ceiling heights of 11 to 14 ft. Thus, the collection is seen in a special and intimate way.

The new rooms match the collection in workmanship and scale. Plasterwork details are of a complexity not usually thought possible today. Finishes include bronze railings, marble bases, and Versailles pattern oak parquet floors.

Technical Requirements

Technical requirements for the galleries are as follows:

- Proper lighting (elimination of ultraviolet portions of the spectrum—25 to 35 footcandles on organic materials)

- Exact temperature and humidity control (+/– 70° Fahrenheit and 50 percent relative humidity)

- Proper security (motion detection/microwave systems and video)

Mechanical details are concealed in the following ways:

- Return grilles are above a wood lattice in the soffit of the small, low passageways that connect the main galleries.

- Display cases and vitrines are openable, but locks and hinges are difficult to detect.

View of Early Bronzes Gallery.
Photo: Stan Ries

SPECIALIZED MUSEUMS AND GALLERIES

Plan of Linsky Galleries.
1 *Entry*
2 *Early bronzes*
3 *Meissen Gallery*
4 *Salon*
5 *Jewelry*
6 *Later bronzes*
7 *Porcelains*

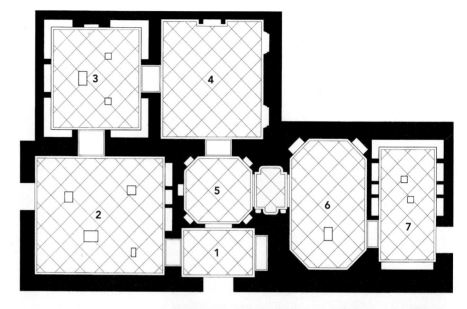

View looking toward Later
Bronzes Gallery.
Photo: Stan Ries

View of salon from entry.
Photo: Stan Ries

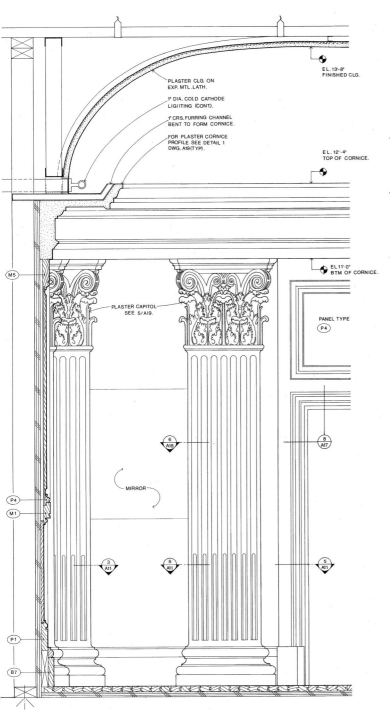

PLASTER CLG. ON
EXP. MTL. LATH.

1" DIA. COLD CATHODE
LIGHTING (CONT).

1" CRS. FURRING CHANNEL
BENT TO FORM CORNICE.

FOR PLASTER CORNICE
PROFILE SEE DETAIL 1
DWG. A19(TYP).

E L.13'-8'
FINISHED CLG.

E L. 12'-4"
TOP OF CORNICE.

EL 11'-0"
BTM OF CORNICE.

PLASTER CAPITOL
SEE 5/A19.

PANEL TYPE
P4

MIRROR

M5
P4
M1
P1
B7

6
A18

8
A17

3
A11

8
A11

5
A11

Detail of the main entrance.
The pilasters framing the
mirrored panel are of wood
with carved plaster capitals.

Detail of cornice at Jewelry
Gallery.

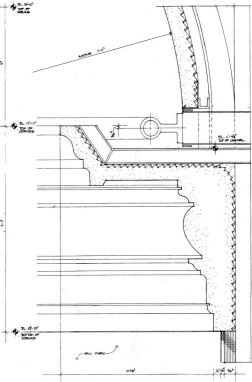

RADIUS 1'-11'

EL. 13'-0'
TOP OF
CEILING

EL. 11'-11"
TOP OF
CORNICE

EL. 11'-11"
TOP OF CHANNEL

EL. 10'-10'
BOTTOM OF
CORNICE

WALL FABRIC

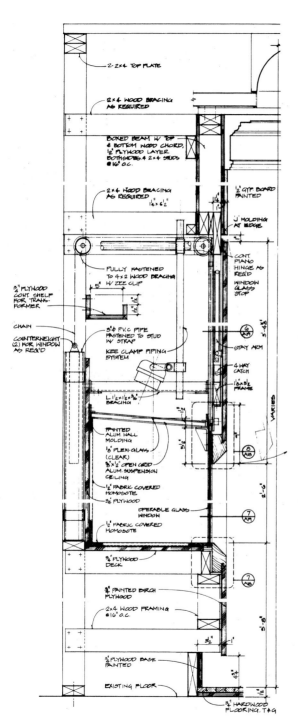

2-2×4 TOP PLATE

2×4 WOOD BRACING AS REQUIRED

BOXED BEAM W/ TOP & BOTTOM WOOD CHORD, 1½" PLYWOOD LAYER BOTH SIDES, 4 2×4 STUDS @ 16" O.C.

2×4 WOOD BRACING AS REQUIRED 1½"×6½"

½" GYP. BOARD PAINTED

"J" MOLDING AT EDGE

CONT. PIANO HINGE AS REQ'D

FULLY FASTENED TO 4×2 WOOD BRACING W/ ZEE CLIP 5"

WINDOW GLASS STOP

¾" PLYWOOD CONT. SHELF FOR TRANS- FORMER

CHAIN

COUNTERWEIGHT (2) FOR WINDOW AS REQ'D

3"Ø P.V.C PIPE FASTENED TO STUD W/ STRAP

KEE CLAMP PIPING SYSTEM

STAY ARM

4 WAY CATCH

1½"×1½" FRAME

L 1½"×1½"×¾" BRACING

PAINTED ALUM WALL MOLDING

⅛" PLEXI-GLASS (CLEAR)

⅜"×2" OPEN GRID ALUM. SUSPENSION CEILING

½" FABRIC COVERED HOMOSOTE

¾" PLYWOOD

OPERABLE GLASS WINDOW

½" FABRIC COVERED HOMOSOTE

¾" PLYWOOD DECK

¾" PAINTED BIRCH PLYWOOD

2×4 WOOD FRAMING @ 16" O.C.

¾" PLYWOOD BASE PAINTED

EXISTING FLOOR

¾" HARDWOOD FLOORING. T&G

◄ Typical detail and section of recessed wall display units. Note attic space for light fixtures, allowing independent relamping without disturbing installed art.

▼ Interior of Later Bronzes Gallery with gold damask wall covering.
Photo: Stan Ries

▲ View of salon; note guardrail.
Photo: Stan Ries

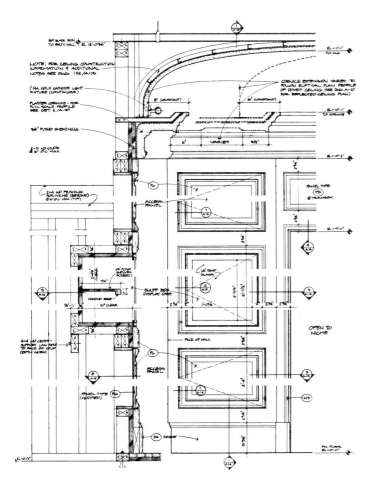

◀ Section and elevation;
snuff box display.

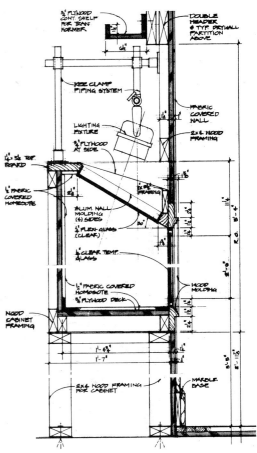

▲ Section through typical
wall case.

◀ Meissen Gallery wall
cases with open light fixture
access panel.
Photo: Stan Ries

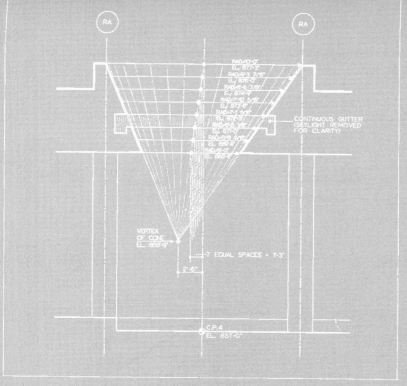

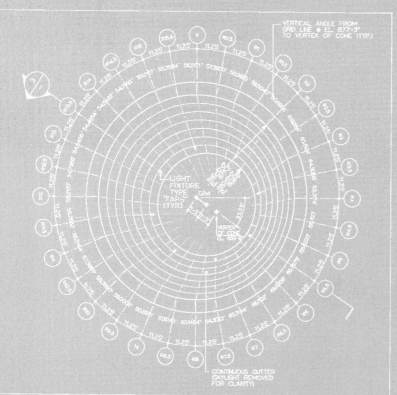

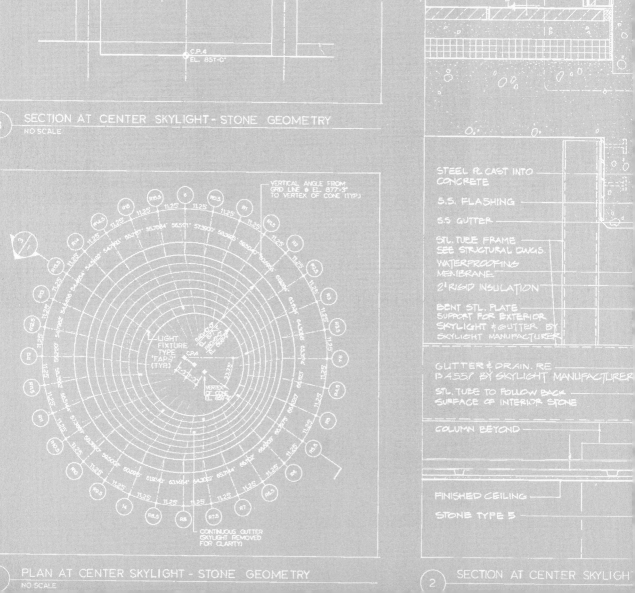

TECHNICAL NOTES

LIGHTING

The goal of architectural and display lighting is to provide an environment that meets both the visual needs of the museum visitor and the conservation needs of the collection.

Lighting should:

- Help to establish the context and style of the building by embellishing important architectural details while seeking to elicit an emotional response from the visitor

- Recognize that a space intended to be perceived as grand or romantic involves a different approach from one designed as efficient or modern

- Incorporate incandescent sources for their color and ability to highlight objects and surfaces, and fluorescent sources for their longevity and efficiency

Entrances

One should feel a sense of excitement when entering a museum. Reduced light levels in the entrance/reception area allow visitors to suddenly notice intriguing spaces nearby. Highlighting some surfaces and leaving others less bright establishes an intuitive wayfinding system to guide museum goers along determined paths.

Galleries

Proper illumination for viewing art and other exhibits can be accomplished in a number of ways. All should establish a comfortable balance between ambient and direct lighting:

- Ambient lighting is general illumination or "fill" light. Light fills a space, such as that from diffused daylight, illuminated coffers (decorative sunken panels in ceilings, domes, or vaults), deep light wells, diffused ceiling slots and skylights, or evenly spaced wall washers surrounding a room.

- Direct lighting is most commonly achieved by the use of flexible track-mounted adjusted accent lights. Recessed fixtures can be used but are more complicated to adjust.

Recommended Maximum Illumination Levels

(measured light striking a display surface)
1 footcandle = 1 lumen = 10.76 lux

Objects Sensitive to Light: 50 lux or 5 footcandles

- Textiles, tapestries, costumes
- Watercolors, prints, and drawings
- Manuscripts
- Miniatures
- Paintings in distemper media
- Wallpapers
- Gouache
- Dyed leather
- Most natural history exhibits, including botanical specimens, fur, and feathers

Objects Less Sensitive to Light: 200 lux or 20 footcandles

- Oil and tempera paintings
- Undyed leather
- Horn, bone, and ivory
- Oriental lacquer

Objects Insensitive to Light: 300 lux or 30 footcandles

These objects may be exposed to higher levels of illumination, but excessive heat is a danger:

- Metal
- Stone
- Glass
- Ceramics
- Jewelry
- Enamel

Incandescent Lamps

Incandescent reflector lamps such as PAR and AR (parabolic and aluminum reflectors) are almost always the most successful means of providing direct light. Beam spreads can be manipulated by using spread lenses, either frosted or prismatic. Louvers reduce glare.

Fluorescent Lamps

Fluorescent sources possess the advantages of long life and easy maintenance. They are most often used for ambient lighting.

Ultraviolet and Infrared Lighting

Considerations in the possible use of ultraviolet(UV) and infrared lighting are as follows:

- Although invisible to the human eye, the risk of damage to sensitive art by UV light is considerable.

- Standard incandescent sources emit little UV light.

- Quartz halogen incandescents provide somewhat more UV light than standard incandescent sources.

- Glass, such as that found on the face of PAR (parabolic aluminum reflector) lamps, absorbs the majority of UV rays, making the lamps acceptable for most installations without the use of UV filters.

- Curators wishing to remove 99 percent of UV rays can request the use of filters, most often placed within the incandescent fixtures.

- Fluorescent sources contain more UV light than incandescent sources and should not be allowed to deliver light without passing through a highly rated UV filter or being reflected off a surface, such as a ceiling, before striking on display surface.

All systems of light delivery should be designed to remove UV rays.

MECHANICAL/ELECTRICAL AND ENVIRONMENTAL SYSTEMS

Critical Conservation Environments

The following standards are critical to conserving collections:

- Systems that serve spaces for the following should be designed for maximum stability of temperature and humidity:
  - Galleries
  - Registrar
  - Preparation

- Collection conservation
- Collection storage

- Space conditions should be maintained at 70°F and 50 percent relative humidity year-round. The system should introduce the minimum outside air required by occupancy, pretreated to conservation conditions—temperature and relative humidity requirements—and delivered via an independent outside air pretreatment system.

- Systems should be designed to operate 365 days a year, 24 hours a day.

- Special attention should be directed to the temperature and relative humidity requirements for photographs, metals, and other works on paper for spaces where lower temperature and/or humidity may be necessary.

- Offices and other general support areas where artwork may be present should be maintained at 75°F with a maximum of 55 percent relative humidity (RH) year-round.

Air System Standards

The following standards should be maintained for air systems:

Area	Environment	Schedule in Hours
Art storage	70°F	24
	50 percent RH	24
Registrar	70°F	24
	50 percent RH	24
Education	75°F	10
	60 percent RH max.	10
Restaurant (food service)	75°F	10
	60 percent RH	10
Kitchen	80°F	10
Reception areas	70°F	24
	50 percent RH	10

Area	Environment	Schedule in Hours
Auditorium	75°F	10
	60 percent RH max.	10
Galleries	70°F	24
	50 percent RH	24
Administration (offices)	75°F	10
	60 percent RH max.	10
Conservation	70°F	24
	50 percent RH	24

SECURITY

Security for a museum should be controlled from a central security panel located in the security office and operated in conjunction with a central security operator's console.

The security system should use the following subsystems and devices:

- Closed circuit television (CCTV), both internal and external
- Magnetic door contacts
- Motion detectors
- Card readers or similar access-control system
- Infrared door shunts
- Electric door strikes
- Guard tour stations
- Panic alarms

The system should also use

- Pagers
- Two-way radios
- Intercom and telephone communications

The central system should monitor, record, and process information accumulated by the system on

- Local printers
- Tape drives
- Videotape
- Computer hard disc

The system should be served by emergency power and have a dedicated, uninterruptable power supply.

It should be capable of being monitored from off-site locations.

FIRE PROTECTION

Museums should be protected by a combination of fire standpipes and sprinklers. The building should be fully sprinklered and contain hazard zones such as book storage, archives, and other areas of risk, including galleries, art storage, and the like.

Generally, the building should be served by a conventional wet pipe sprinkler system. Where there is no danger of damage to the collection from an accidental discharge, a double interlock preaction type of system should be used. Systems known as flo-control sprinklers can also be used in high-risk areas.

GLOSSARY

air lock An airtight chamber or enclosure, usually located between two regions of unequal temperature, humidity, or pressure, in which these conditions can be regulated.

baffle A device that regulates the flow of fluid, air, or light.

brise-soleil An arrangement of horizontal or vertical fins to shade window openings.

cantilever A horizontal projection, such as a step, balcony, beam, or canopy, that is held in place without external bracing and appears to be self-supporting.

caryatid A sculptured female figure used as a column to support an entablature or other similar member. The term is also applied to various other columns or pilasters carved wholly or partly in the form of a human figure.

circulation loop A means of unhindered passage through a building, such as a foyer, corridor, stairway, or elevator.

clerestory A window admitting light to the interior of a building that is installed on an exterior wall contiguous to a roof.

coffer A decorative recessed panel in a vault, ceiling, or soffit.

condition report A report on the physical condition of a work of art or other object that is prepared by a curator, registrar, or conservator. It is usually accompanied by a photographic record.

cornice Any projecting ornamental molding along the top of a building, wall, or arch.

cove A concave moulding produced by the arched junction of wall and ceiling.

curvilinear Consisting of or bounded by curved lines; following a curve.

docent A teacher or lecturer who is not a regular museum staff member.

double glazing Two layers of glass set in a window to reduce heat flow in either direction.

enfilade The French system of aligning internal doors in a sequence so that a vista is obtained when all the doors are open. The arrangement was introduced in 1650 and became a feature of Baroque palace planning.

fiber optics The mechanics or optics of light transmission through very fine, flexible glass rods by internal reflection.

footprint The outline of a building or structure on a site.

footcandle The illumination of a surface 1 ft away from a source of one candle, equal to 1 lumen per sq ft.

helicoidal Having the form of a flat coil or flattened spiral.

infrared Electromagnetic radiation having wavelengths greater than those of visible light and shorter than those of microwaves.

International Style A term coined in the United States in the 1930s referring to new architectural styles being created by architects such as Le Corbusier, Adolph Loos, and Walter Gropius.

kiasma (or chiasma) A biological term for the intersection or crossing over of two tracts, such as nerves or ligaments, in an X shape. Kiasma is used by Steven Holl to describe his Museum for Contemporary Art in Helsinki, Finland, as a structure that intersects with culture, nature, and the urban grid.

lantern A small circular or polygonal turret with windows all around, crowning a roof or dome.

loading dock A raised platform used for loading or unloading wheeled freight carriers such as trucks or railway cars.

louver A framed opening in a wall, fitted with fixed or movable slanted slats.

lumen A unit of light emitted by a uniform point source of one candle. The term is used in measuring the level of light on surfaces of art and other objects, and on walls, ceilings, and floors.

lunette A semicircular opening or any flat semicircular surface.

lux Used in the international system of measuring illumination; 1 lux is equal to 1 lumen per square meter.

museology The science or profession of museum organization, equipment, and management.

oculus A circular opening in a wall or at the apex of a dome.

photoelectric cell An electronic device that responds to visible light.

porte cochere A carriage entrance leading to a courtyard or entrance to a structure.

portland limestone A yellowish-white building limestone from the Isle of Portland, a peninsula in southern England.

registrar A person responsible for development and enforcement of policies and procedures concerning the acquisition, management, and disposition of collections. This person also arranges for accessions, loans, and the packing and shipping of museum materials.

single-span vault A vaulted space without intermediate supports.

skyway An overhead pedestrian bridge.

space frame A three-dimensional framework for enclosing spaces, in which all structural members are interconnected and act as a single entity; usually applied to the enclosure of column-free large spaces.

stepped back Designed so that successive stories or groups of stories recede farther and farther from the front, side, or rear of a building.

tectonic Pertaining to construction or building; architectural.

tie rod A rod used as a connecting member or brace.

titanium A strong, low-density, highly corrosion-resistant, lustrous white metallic element that occurs widely in igneous rocks and is used primarily to alloy aircraft metals for low weight, strength, and high-temperature stability. Architect Frank Gehry has used titanium extensively as a cladding for buildings.

torsion The condition of being twisted or turned; the stress caused when one end of an object is twisted in one direction and the other end is motionless or twisted in an opposite direction.

torus A convex moulding of semicircular profile.

truncated cylinder A cylindrical section lacking an apex or point and terminating in a plane—a flat surface parallel to the base.

ultraviolet Light wavelengths beyond the violet in the visible spectrum. The ultraviolet part of the spectrum can be injurious to patinated or applied surfaces and to organic and inorganic materials.

wall washer A light fixture designed to illuminate large vertical surfaces or walls.

water garden A garden in which aquatic plants predominate; a garden built around a stream or pool as a central feature.

BIBLIOGRAPHY

American Association of Museums. *The Accessible Museum: Model Programs of Accessibility for Disabled and Older People.* Washington, D.C.: American Association of Museums, 1992.

———. *Caring for Collections: Strategies for Conservation, Maintenance, Documentation.* Washington, D.C.: American Association of Museums, 1984.

———. *Introduction to Museum Evaluation.* New York: American Association of Museums/Committee on Audience Research and Evaluation (CARE), 1999.

———. *Standard Facility Report.* 2d ed. revised. Washington, D.C.: American Association of Museums/Registrars Committee of the AAM, 1998.

Appelbaum, Barbara. *Guide to Environmental Protection of Collections.* Sound View Press, 1991.

Belcher, Michael. *Exhibitions in Museums.* Washington, D.C.: Smithsonian Institution Press, 1991.

Buck, Rebecca A. ed. and Jean Allman Gilmore. *The New Museum Registration Methods.* 4th ed. Washington, D.C.: American Association of Museums.

Cassar, May. *Environmental Management: Guidelines for Museum and Galleries.* New York: Routledge, 1995.

Caulton, Tim. *Hands-On Exhibitions: Managing Interactive Museums and Science Centres.* New York: Routledge, 1998.

Chenhall, Robert G. and David Vance. *Museum Collections and Today's Computers.* New York: Greenwood Press, 1988.

Dana, John Cotton. *The New Museum: Selected Writings.* Washington, D.C.: American Association of Museums/The Newark Museum Association, 1999.

Darragh, Joan and James S. Snyder. *Museum Design: Planning and Building for Art.* New York: Oxford University Press/The American Federation of Arts and the National Endowment for the Arts, 1993.

Dean, David. *Museum Exhibition: Theory and Practice.* New York: Routledge, 1994.

Edson, Gary and David Dean. *Handbook for Museums.* New York: Routledge, 1994.

Ellis, Margaret Holben. *The Care of Prints and Drawings.* Nashville, Tenn.: American Association for State and Local History, 1987.

Fahy, Anne, ed. *Collections Management.* New York: Routledge, 1995.

Falk, John H. and Lynn D. Dierking. *The Museum Experience.* Whalesback Books, 1992.

Fox, Michael J. and Peter L. Wikerson. *Introduction to Archival Organization and Description.* Los Angeles, Calif.: Getty Trust Publications, 1999.

Graubard, Stephen R., ed. "America's Museums." *Daedalus* Vol. 128, no. 3 (Summer 1999).

Groff, Gerda and Laura Gardner. *What Museums Need to Know: Access for Blind and Visually Impaired Visitors.* American Foundation for the Blind Press, 1993.

Hein, George E. *Learning in the Museum.* New York: Routledge, 1998.

Hooper-Greenhill, Eilean, ed. *The Educational Role of the Museum.* 2d ed. New York: Routledge, 1994.

———. *Museums and the Shaping of Knowledge.* New York: Routledge, 1992.

———. *Museums and Their Visitors.* New York: Routledge, 1994.

IESNA Committee on Museum and Art Gallery Lighting. *Museum and Art Gallery Lighting: A Recommended Practice.* The Illuminating Engineering Society of North America, 1996.

Kay, Gersil N. *Fiber Optics in Architectural Lighting: Methods, Design, and Applications.* New York: McGraw-Hill, 1999.

Knell, Simon, ed. *Care of Collections.* New York: Routledge, 1994.

BIBLIOGRAPHY

Liston, David, ed. *Museum Security and Protection: A Handbook for Cultural Heritage Institutions.* New York: International Committee on Museum Security and Routledge, 1993.

Malaro, Marie C. *Museum Governance: Mission, Ethics, Policy.* Washington, D.C.: Smithsonian Institution Press, 1994.

Ogden, Sherelyn. *Preservation Planning: Guidelines for Writing a Long-Range Plan.* Washington, D.C.: American Association of Museums/Northeast Document Conservation Center, 1998.

Pitman, Bonnie, ed. *Presence of Mind: Museums and the Spirit of Learning.* Washington, D.C.: American Association of Museums, 1999.

Schultz, Arthur W, ed. *Caring for Your Collections.* New York: Harry N. Abrams, 1992.

Serrell, Beverly. *Paying Attention: Visitors and Museum Exhibitions.* Washington D.C.: American Association of Museums, 1998.

Theoobald, Mary Miley. *Museum Store Management.* Nashville, Tenn.: AltaMira Press/American Association for State and Local History, 1991.

Thomson, Garry. *The Museum Environment.* 2d ed. Boston, Mass.: Butterworth, 1986.

Zorich, Diane M. *Introduction to Managing Digital Assets: Options for Cultural and Educational Organizations.* Los Angeles, Calif.: Getty Trust Publications, 1999.

INDEX

BUILDING TYPE BASICS FOR MUSEUMS:

1. Program (predesign)
What are the principal programming requirements (space types and areas)? How do you organize the client?
2, 6, 14, 16, 32, 36, 39, 40–41, 43, 44, 48, 50–51, 58, 60, 68, 78, 80, 83, 89, 101, 118, 124, 138, 141, 154, 161–62, 167, 177, 183–84, 187–88, 191, 198, 204, 208–9, 214, 216, 221–22, 228, 233, 242

2. Circulation
What are the desirable primary and secondary spatial relationships?
2, 8, 13–14, 17–23, 32, 40–42, 48, 63, 66–67, 70–74, 77–78, 80, 82, 86–88, 90–92, 94, 108–11, 113, 114, 116–18, 120, 130, 132–34, 136, 142, 144–46, 148, 150, 154, 157–59, 160, 164, 166–69, 172–74, 179–80, 184, 190, 192–95, 201–2, 204, 207, 210, 214, 216, 217, 219, 224–25, 228

3. Unique design concerns
What special design determinants must be considered? Design process? Obsolescence? Security?
2, 8, 14, 18–19, 32, 36, 48, 60–61, 68, 76, 78, 80–81, 89, 101–2, 104–6, 112, 118, 120, 126, 138, 140, 154, 156, 162, 165, 166, 177, 180, 183–86, 198, 200, 206, 211, 214, 220–21, 228, 235, 242, 252

4. Site planning/parking/access
What considerations determine external access and parking?
2, 4–5, 14, 32, 35, 38, 40, 48, 50–51, 60, 62, 90, 101–3, 118, 122–24, 126–27, 130, 138, 154, 156, 162, 164–65, 178, 184, 198, 200, 204, 223, 230, 232–34, 242

5. Codes/ADA
Which building codes and regulations apply, and what are the main applicable provisions? (Examples: egress; electrical; plumbing; ADA; seismic; asbestos and other hazards)
252

6. Energy/environmental challenges
What are the techniques to use in obtaining appropriate energy conservation and environmental sustainability?
27, 40, 239, 251–52

7. Structure system
What are the appropriate structural systems to consider?
2, 32, 98, 124, 164, 177, 214

8. Mechanical systems
What are the appropriate systems for heating, ventilating, and air-conditioning (hvac) and plumbing? Vertical transportation? What factors affect preliminary selection? What are the space requirements?
101, 177, 182, 201, 241–42, 251–52

9. Electrical/communications
What are the appropriate systems for electrical, voice, and data communications? What considerations affect preliminary selection? What are the space requirements?
241, 251